The Authorities

Powerful Wisdom from Leaders in the Field

GLENN EDWARDS

Award Winning Author

AuthoritiesPress

Dedicated in memory to my heroes, Uncle Arnold and Aunt Donna.

FOREWORD

Experts are to be admired for their knowledge, but they often remain unrecognized by the general public because they save their information and insights for paying customers and clients. There are many experts in a given field, but their impact is limited to the handful of people with whom they work.

Unlike experts, authorities share their knowledge and expertise far more broadly, so they make a big impact on the world. Authorities become known and admired as leading experts and, as such, typically do very well economically and professionally. Most authorities are also mature enough to know that part of the joy of monetary success is the accompanying moral and spiritual obligation to give back.

Many people want to learn and work with well-respected and generous authorities, but don't always know where to find them. They may be known to their peers, or within a specific community, but have not had the opportunity to reach a wider audience. At one time, they might have submitted a proposal to the *For Dummies* or *Chicken Soup for the Soul* series of books, but it's now almost impossible to get accepted as a new author in such branded book series.

It is more than fitting that Raymond Aaron, an internationally known and respected authority in his own right, would be the one to recognize the need for a new venue in which authorities could share their considerable knowledge with readers everywhere. As the only author ever to be included in both of the book series mentioned above, Raymond has had the opportunity to give back and he understands how crucial it is for authorities to have a platform from which to share their expertise.

I have known and worked with Raymond for a number of years and consider him a valued friend and talented coach. He knows how to spot talented and knowledgeable people and he desires to see them prosper. Over the years, success coaching and speaking engagements around the world have made it possible for Raymond to meet many of these talented authorities. He recognizes and relates to their passion and enthusiasm for what they do, as well as their desire to share what they know. He tells me that's why he created this new nonfiction branded book series, *The Authorities*.

Dr. Nido Qubein
President, High Point University

TABLE OF CONTENTS

INTRODUCTION

Welcome to *The Authorities*. This is an anthology of stories and ideas from individuals who have distinguished themselves in life and in business. They are people who leave big footprints on the world, and as leaders in their particular fields they also understand the importance and obligation of giving something back.

Authorities are not just experts. They are also known to be outstanding in their fields and in their communities. Because of this important difference, authorities are able to contribute more to humanity through both their chosen work and by giving back.

You will definitely know some of *The Authorities* in this book, especially since there are some world-famous ones. Others are just as exceptional, but you may not yet know about them.

Our featured author is Glenn Edwards. Glenn is a passionate speaker and storyteller, an entrepreneur with two successful businesses under his belt, an amazing father, an incredible grandfather, and a loving partner. The things in life that mean the most to him are not in what he is able to accomplish in this world, but who he is able to inspire.

Glenn shares his true story in the hope that it will reach those who need it most. Having experienced heartbreak, loss, and trauma he is no stranger to the negative thoughts and emotions these events cause. Yet, he has made the conscious choice to choose positivity. He believes that there is a positive to be found in every situation we face in life; we just have to open ourselves up to see it.

When Glenn began to seek help for the rage that had built up inside him, he found it difficult to find the help he needed within a system that doesn't always listen. He believes that people do in fact care; you just have to find those that are ready to truly listen and provide you with the help you need. In order to do this you have to first understand what you need and, second, advocate for yourself.

Through both his speaking and his writing, Glenn emphasizes the importance of healing in order to live a positive and fulfilling life. When you choose to heal you allow yourself the opportunity to find joy in your life again. When you choose to heal you take your power back. Glenn is an advocate for the power of positive thinking, and he inspires his audience to empower themselves, through healing and self-love, to live the life they desire.

To learn more about Glenn or to connect with him about speaking at your next event, visit **glennedwards.ca**

We suggest you read each chapter carefully to learn and to see the business possibilities that may exist between yourself and any of the authorities. You could become their client or, perhaps, do business with them in other ways.

These are *The Authorities*. Learn from them. Connect with them. Let them uplift you. Learning from them and working with them is a secret ingredient for success which may well allow you to rise to the level of Authority yourself soon.

To be considered for inclusion in a subsequent edition of *The Authorities*, register to attend an event at www.aaron.com/events where you will be interviewed and considered.

ACKNOWLEDGEMENTS

I am so incredibly grateful for the love of my life, **Paula**. She is a beautiful person both inside and out. If it weren't for her, I may have overlooked this opportunity. She reminded me that, just like when I chose to walk away from my pro hockey career, I was at a fork in the road. I could choose to pursue my passion for speaking and writing, or I could walk away from it.

Thank you **Paula,** for inspiring me to go for it. Thank you for inspiring me every day with your determination, passion, and love. You are a true gift. I don't feel that I can even capture in words how you make this world a better place.

Dr. David MacQuarrie, thank you for saving my life. Your willingness to fight the system and work with each client individually is remarkable and courageous. You took the time and care to develop a successful treatment plan that gave me the tools I need for ongoing growth and healing.

Thank you to **Raymond Aaron** and **James McNeil** for your support. You both have motivated me to embrace this new passion. You've helped me see that it is possible, and for that I am grateful.

Thank you to **Andreah Barker** for taking the time to not only hear me, but to truly listen.

From Pain to Powerful

GLENN EDWARDS

"You have the power to heal your life, and you need to know that. We think so often that we are helpless, but we're not. We always have the power of our minds... Claim and consciously use your power."

– Louise L. Hay

YOU ARE YOUR POWER

When all goes wrong, how do you use your power to heal?

When you feel like you have no fight left, how do you call on your power to lift you up?

When you think you can't take any more, how do you remind yourself that

1

you do have power?

I have learned a lot in this lifetime, as we all do when we're open to the lesson. But I believe the most important one is that I always have the power to heal. It is a choice and it's my choice. The same goes for you too. YOU HAVE A CHOICE. You can either let anger, regret, loss, disappointment, and fear steal your power away, or you can use your power to heal.

It's on you! Make the choice to live in your misery or do the work. It took me a while to learn this lesson. Now that I have, I can't unlearn it. I have actively made the choice to not only live in positivity, but to be a positive light for others as well. Don't get me wrong here, the fact that I choose to be positive doesn't mean that I don't recognize or deal with my negative emotions. They are there. I feel them. Some of them are the effect of a cause that's based in reality and some of them are born out of anxiety. They exist. I do the work to turn them around.

Positivity isn't magic. It's not a mythical creature in a story with a fairy-tale ending. You can create your own happily(ish)-ever-after. I know it because I've done it and my life is no stranger to tragedy. Oh and I say happily(ish) because, let's be real here, the whole idea of happily-ever-after is misleading. It leads the audience to assume that everything from that point on was perfection, but life will never be perfect. There will always be challenges. There will always be work to do. Living with a positive outlook isn't about arriving at a destination, it's a continuous exploration. It's one that I am excited to embark on every single day.

LOSING MYSELF

Like I said, I am no stranger to tragedy and loss. My family has lived through the double homicide of my aunt and uncle, drug addiction, rape, divorce (she just walked away after 33 years), and the alienation of my 5 grandchildren.

As these things were happening to me and all around me, I suppressed my emotions. I was that guy: the confident one who could walk into a room and make others laugh. I had grown two successful businesses and was an inspiration to others who wanted to do the same. I loved to goof off and joke around. All the while I was dying on the inside. I hated the word negative and actually still do, but my relationship with the word has changed. Before I began to work on myself, I suppressed my negative emotions, allowing them to fester and grow. Now I deal with them, and use my power to heal. It is in the healing that I have become a more positive, joyful, and abundant person.

What changed? What made me realize I needed help? What was my turning point?

It was that moment when I realized I had lost myself so completely and entirely that I had created an exit plan. I was ready to die. I was ready to commit suicide. I had hit a point where everything felt like too much. I was overwhelmed by anger and sadness. The hurt that I had been suppressing for years had bubbled to the surface, causing an uncontrollable rage within me that was coming out in ways that made me feel like someone else entirely. I had lost myself in it.

Even in those moments when I was ready to kill myself, I realized it wasn't right. I never, ever thought that I would want that. I knew I had so much to be grateful for in my life and yet I couldn't see past the horrible things that had happened not only to myself, but the people I loved.

Until one day, a realization broke through the noise. It was a whisper at first and I almost didn't even hear it. It said, "You don't actually want to die. You have so much life left. Are you really ready to miss out on all this world has left to offer you?"

I am now so incredibly grateful that I heard the whisper. If I hadn't, I wouldn't be here today to understand just how much I would've left behind. That one powerful thought made me realize that I was the only one who could turn things around. I had to make the choice to pick myself up, seek the help I needed and do the work to heal.

I've done the work and continue to do the work.

MY life is worth it and so am I.

YOUR life is worth it and so are you.

OWN YOUR POWER

Owning the power within yourself begins with accepting all that you are. This acceptance will allow you to recognize the aspects of you that you love and want to strengthen, while helping you also to understand the aspects of your personality that you don't love and want to work on. No one is perfect. No one makes all the right decisions. Accept your flaws and know that, no matter what, you are a work in progress, one that is worth the effort.

One of the results of not working on my emotional responses to the external circumstances I faced daily was rage. Years of repression caught up with me and manifested in a lack of emotional control. I couldn't contain my anger. There was too much that had built up over time. It began exploding out of me. I didn't like it. It didn't feel good. It made me feel less than the person I had always thought I was. It diminished my power.

Once I made the choice to live, I knew that my life depended on me dealing with my pain. The time to face it had come. I knew I needed help, and as I learned throughout the process, it was important to seek the right kind of help. The first step for me was to deal with my rage.

I had been to visit my daughter, who had been battling drug addiction and was in rehab, when it hit me. If she had the strength she needed to beat drugs, then I too could beat my rage and live a more positive life.

I began my search for help by going to my doctor and explaining what my emotional outbursts felt like. He immediately referred me to meet with a social worker. It was completely unacceptable. The social worker couldn't even begin to comprehend the level of help I required. My case was over his head, and so I had to go back to my doctor and advocate for my needs.

He then sent me to a psychiatrist who worked with rage. If you don't know exactly what rage is, that's okay. You really don't want to. There are two types of rage: explosion and implosion. I was experiencing the explosive version and it was not pretty. If the line was crossed, really, really bad things, such as years or possibly a lifetime of jail, could happen. I worked so hard not to cross that line.

The first psychiatrist I met with purposely tried to instigate a rage, so that he could capture it on camera. What?!? I was floored. Did he not understand? He was the only one in the room with me. Did he really think he could control me? I didn't want to find out. I wanted help, and his methods were only serving to make things worse. Even the second psychiatrist, his partner, couldn't understand why he would do this.

It took me a few more tries to find the psychiatrist that worked for me and who ultimately gave me the tools I needed to continue to work on myself. My point in telling you this story is that you really need to make sure the help you need is the help you're getting. Although it may feel like an overwhelming challenge when you're not feeling well, you have to be a strong advocate for yourself.

One of the most worrisome aspects of the healthcare system, the way it is set up today, is that there seems to be little to no accountability, especially within the area of mental health. What this means is that often psychiatrists do not have the skills to treat all of the patients they are presented with. In my case, I found that they would hear me, but not necessarily listen to me, and then at the end of it all they would say there was nothing they could do for me. What a colossal waste of time! Not only that, but it was incredibly disheartening.

What I've learned to do is ask the psychiatrist flat out if they can handle my case. I let them know how important it is that they not take me on if they can't help. I let them know it's okay if they can't help and ask them to research and recommend a specialist who can.

People need to slow down and listen. If you feel you're not being heard then you need to find someone who will listen to you, and I mean authentically listen to your individual story and personalized needs. ADVOCATE FOR YOURSELF!

Understanding and working through my emotions in order to control my rage was only a small part of the work I did to turn my life around. I also sought the expertise of life coaches, like Raymond Aaron, who have helped me realize that, while I do have a fulfilling life, I am still playing small. I could be doing more.

While I write this chapter I am fast approaching my 60th birthday. Not everyone thinks that, at this age, it's time to achieve new goals. I do. Changing my perspective from being one that was stuck in negativity to one that is now filled with positivity has opened up a whole new world of possibility. I am ready to embark on this new adventure and share my journey with you, all because I decided that I wasn't ready to give up on my life. In doing this, I began to truly own my power in a way that I have never done so before.

Some of the lessons I learned on my own healing journey that I would like to share with the world are:

1. Know your core values.

2. Communication is key.

3. Accept yourself and treat yourself with compassion.

4. Forgive yourself for letting things go.

5. You have to heal in order to recover.

6. There is always a positive.

7. Be transparent.

8. The best place to live is in your dash.

9. It is never too late to live your best life.

KNOW YOUR CORE VALUES

Do you know your core values? You know, the ones you live by. The ones that help you make the tough decisions. The ones that keep you on that life path that is uniquely yours.

I have found that most people don't. When I ask people I get a range of responses from I don't think about that stuff to oh, I dunno... to yeah, I guess it would be something like love and honesty.

A lot of people really don't sit down to think about their core values. I mean really think about them, define them, and understand how living by them can truly change their life. Your core values are a bit like those signs that let you know where to turn when you're headed towards the airport. Heading to the airport? Yes, turn right in 500 meters. Perfect! Now you know exactly where you're going.

Why wouldn't you want to know what your core values are? They are essentially your internal road map, especially during the really bad times when it's easy to veer off course. I've done the work to define my core values and it has helped immensely in not only healing my past pain, but in helping me deal with hurt as it happens in the moment.

How do you know what your core values are? Take some time and think about what means most to you in your life. Is it love? Is it health? Is it creativity? Is it discovery? Your core values are unique to you, and no book can tell you exactly what they are. That is something you have to decide for yourself.

The top 6 core values that guide me are:

- Honesty
- Compassion
- Integrity
- Clarity
- Calm
- Fun

Once you have a general idea, you need to go deeper. For example, what exactly do I mean by honesty? Sure, it seems simple: always tell the truth. I'm almost 100% sure everyone reading this learned how to tell a lie very early in life, especially when busted doing something their parents had specifically told them not to. Go deeper than that! For me, honesty means not only being honest with others, but being honest with myself.

It is so easy to lie to myself. I am brilliant at it! Or, I used to be anyway. Now, I look a little more closely. A simple example: I lost $300 dollars at the casino in 20 minutes a few months back. Ouch! I quickly reached for my wallet, telling myself I could easily make it back.

What a liar! Obviously, I couldn't easily make it back or I wouldn't have lost it in the first place. The truth is that gambling, being a game of chance, offered me the opportunity to win it back, but only if I was willing to lose more money. I wasn't. I put my wallet back where it belonged!

Go through each core value and flesh it out. These are your guides. They will keep you on a life path that brings you more joy and less pain, as long as you let them.

COMMUNICATION IS KEY

Bottling up your feelings and expecting others to understand why you're hurt is one of the best ways to ensure that you will never heal. Communicate your emotions. Talk about your feelings. If you're upset with someone, tell them. Just because you feel something doesn't make it right. You may be completely misinterpreting the other person's words or actions. Ask them why they did it. Ask them what they're feeling. Talk it out.

Three components to open communication:

1.   Honest and authentic sharing.

2.   Active listening.

3.   Coming together.

All can be a challenge. Most people don't share what they have to say because they think no one cares. I disagree. I think the right people care, even if what you're telling them is hard to hear.

You have to be willing to listen to what they have to say too. Communication is never one-sided. If you're speaking and not hearing, you're just talking at someone and you'll never achieve authentic communication. You have to listen actively. That means tuning in with your thoughts while the other person is speaking and making sure you haven't let them wander away from listening. One of the biggest mistakes people make is listening with the intent to respond. This isn't real listening. Listen, just to listen. If you need time to think about your response, that's okay, take what you need. It isn't a movie. There isn't an audience waiting for a snappy reply.

I wish that my daughter would talk to me about why I had to lay off her husband. She's never even tried to talk to me about it. She doesn't want to know why because she doesn't care. This is an example of what happens when communication breaks down. As you can see, even though I've done the work to heal and live with a more positive outlook, life isn't perfect. I still can't reach my daughter, and I miss my grandkids every day.

My daughter's inability to communicate her feelings to me has caused her to use her children as a weapon, which I personally feel is child abuse. It's fine for her to be mad at me. Adults fight. But adults also resolve their issues through sharing their feelings and listening to the other person's side. It hurts. But in order to heal, you have to deal with the hurt. What adults should never do is bring innocent children into the mix of their adult fight. It isn't right. I wish she would just talk to me instead.

ACCEPT YOURSELF AND TREAT YOURSELF WITH COMPASSION

One of hardest things for me to do as I worked on healing was to accept that I was at one time willing to take my own life. I had always seen myself as strong, successful, confident, and filled with an unwavering passion for life. My desire to end it all shook me to my core. How could someone who was proud of living a full life want to give it all up without a fight?

Once I was able to accept that part of myself, I was able to move forward in my own healing. Not only that, but I had to accept my anger, understand why I was angry, and show myself some compassion. It is acceptance combined with compassion that will see you through to the healing you not only need but deserve.

Yes, you deserve to heal. Some of the reasons you might be stopping yourself from healing are:

- You don't want to deal with the pain.

- You are suppressing your emotions in order to not hurt others.

- You are afraid of looking too closely at the cause of your hurt.

- You are uncertain of what a future without the pain will look like.

- You are comfortable living in your misery.

Does any of this sound like you? I know that at one point or another in my life, all of it sounded like me. I lived in my pain and suffering for so long. I got by and still managed on the outside to project a life of success and happiness. That outward projection, as you've seen, couldn't have been more wrong.

Take a moment and understand why you've chosen not to allow yourself to heal from past pain. Think about how it is affecting your life, and about the joy it has stopped you from experiencing. Accept your reasons, show yourself some compassion, and make a promise to yourself to begin the healing process now.

FORGIVE YOURSELF FOR LETTING THINGS GO

Sometimes in order to heal you need to simply let things go without a resolution. The person you feel you need an apology from in order to obtain closure is either unable or unwilling to give it. This may not feel okay, but you have to let it be; otherwise, you are the one who will live the rest of your life feeling that pain.

The man who murdered my aunt and uncle never once apologized. I wanted an apology. Not so that I could forgive him; I don't need to forgive him. I felt like I needed it so that I could move on, especially so that I could let go of the anger that I had been carrying for so long. Long after my cousin went on to live a life her parents would be so proud of. It wasn't until I forgave myself for failing to obtain an apology from her parents' murderer that I was able to begin the healing process. It was in forgiving myself that I was able to live a more positive life.

I know this might not be what you'd expect to hear. Most people might say that they forgave the person who they needed the apology from, but for me, it was myself that I needed to forgive. So forgive yourself for letting yourself down and then let go of your need for the apology that you will never receive.

YOU HAVE TO HEAL IN ORDER TO RECOVER

You can't go over it. You can't get around it. You can't go under it. You can't run through it blindly with your eyes closed, hoping you'll come out the other end without a few scars. You have to walk through your healing process at a pace that allows you to feel all the things you need to feel in order to heal.

Living in the pain of a new wound without the help of a painkiller, or re-opening old wounds hurts. But in order to truly heal from emotional trauma, it has to be done. Whether it is death, the end of a marriage, a traumatic event, a friend who wronged you, an employer who took advantage of you, a seemingly perfect opportunity that passed you by, you have to find a way to heal.

What healing looks like for you won't be the same as what it looks like for anyone else. Compassion, acceptance and forgiveness are all great places to begin, but where do you need to go from there in your healing process? For me it was to deal with my pent up anger. With each new tragedy or loss, I let my rage take over. I had allowed it a lifetime of expansion, and so for me that was the next step in my healing process.

How has your pain held you back? Pain can manifest in feelings of guilt, low self-esteem, anger, self-pity, fear, anxiety, self-hatred… you name the horrible feeling, and your pain has a hand in it. All of these can escalate to depression, suicidal ideation, and even suicide if left to grow within you. Guilt, low self-esteem, and self-hatred can stop you from recognizing new opportunities or even taking action on the opportunities that are right there for your taking because you don't value yourself or your life. All of these feelings make you feel insignificant, and ensure that you will continue living your life small.

Heal your pain; your life depends on it! Your big, expansive, and joy-filled life is waiting.

THERE IS ALWAYS A POSITIVE

Even in the absolute worst of situations there is a positive to be found. Yes, in death, divorce, drug addiction, and traumatic events there is always a positive.

How angry did you feel reading that? Are you ready to throw the book down and call it a day? Are you cursing my name?

Look, I am not saying that you have to turn these events into a positive. I am not one of those faux positive people who glosses over the bad in an attempt to be a positive person. In fact, I am quite the opposite. Faux positivity only serves to bury your emotions. What I am talking about is the part of the healing process when you've recognized that you need to heal, you're ready to embark on the journey, you know how to show yourself the compassion you need, and you've begun to forgive yourself for anything you need to; and so you are ready to open your eyes to all that is there.

Let me share what I mean. A few years back I had to let my son-in-law go from one of my companies. I had received multiple complaints from other staff about his uncontrollable behaviour. I even spoke with him about the issues on more than one occasion. Yet, still he continued. Maybe he thought that his connection to me kept him safe. Unfortunately, he was hurting my business. I couldn't let him continue on with the company.

Do you know how hard it is to let a family member go? The decision didn't come lightly or swiftly. I gave him every opportunity to change, and yet when I finally did have to make the hard call he looked at me and said, "Remember every action has a reaction."

Since that day I haven't been allowed to see my grandchildren.

Am I happy about the situation?

Of course not.

Do I miss them every, single day?

Of course I do.

Would I change what I did to get them back?

No, I did what was right.

Do I still feel angry about it sometimes?

YES!

But... I recognize why I'm angry. It was losing them that drove me over the edge. It was losing them that forced me to want to end my life. It was too much.

Since that time, I have taken steps to heal the pain of the loss, like participating in Facebook groups for alienated grandparents. And most importantly, I have found the positive: for six wonderful years I knew what it felt like to be a grandfather to five beautiful children. It's not an experience everyone on this earth has the pleasure to know, and I did. No one can take those years or those memories away from me. That is my positive in this situation. Having that time with my grandkids is my saving grace. I will be forever grateful for the gift of those memories.

Are you in a situation right now where it's hard to see any sort of positive? Begin to heal yourself on the inside, and the positive will become more visible.

BE TRANSPARENT

If I'm feeling emotional or angry about something, I do my best to be transparent about where my feelings are coming from. For example, if I've had an annoying commute into work and I know I'm grumpy I'll let my staff know that my mood has nothing to do with them.

Some people believe that being an open book can take away your power. This hasn't been my experience. I believe that transparency allows you to own your power. You accept all aspects of yourself and so there's nothing to hide.

Silence hurts.

Silence causes misunderstandings.

Silence makes us think things are worse than they are.

Silence causes arguments to escalate.

Silence causes pain to grow.

Communication has the ability to heal all wounds, as long as both parties are willing to listen. When you are open, honest, and lay everything on the table you allow yourself to be fully seen. You are giving of yourself in a vulnerable yet powerful way by letting everyone in on who you are and why you respond to things the way you do.

If I come home in a bad mood because someone at work upset me but

I don't say anything, my partner could think it's her fault. She can't read my mind. Rather than letting those thoughts fester and cause even more misunderstanding, I would rather let her know why I'm feeling grumpy and let her support me. Only good can come from this.

Communication is everything. Be transparent and watch how your interactions with others improve.

THE BEST PLACE TO LIVE IS IN YOUR DASH

"Your life is made of two dates and a dash. Make the most of the dash."

– Linda Ellis

This quote resonates with me like no other. There is no better place to live than in your dash. It's the place where life exists. It's the place where you get to make your mark in the world. It's the place where you get to experience all the great things this life has to offer you.

If I had chosen to take matters into my own hands and make my second date earlier than it should've been, I would've missed out on so much. With open eyes, I met a woman who inspires me, brings me so much joy, gives her love freely, and accepts me for who I am.

I am so incredibly grateful that I am here to experience this leg of the journey. There is so much richness in my life. I am also so grateful to myself for not giving up on me. I've forgiven myself for wanting to end everything and have done so much work to live in the positive.

Take it from someone who has been on the other side of trauma: no matter what you've been through, you too can live a positive and fulfilling life. You have to do the work! If you want to live your best life, it's time to take on your pain and heal.

Recognize your pain.

Admit you need to change.

Accept yourself.

Forgive yourself.

Communicate.

Find the positive.

Live your best life every single day!

IT'S NEVER TOO LATE TO LIVE YOUR BEST LIFE

"There are powers inside of you which, if you could discover and use, would make of you everything you ever dreamed or imagined you could become."

–Orison Swett Marden

You are your power! Sometimes you need some inspiration to help you head down a positive path. You can make a choice to wallow in your pain, or you can do the work. It's easy to choose not to do the work, but living through each day will be hard.

It's never too late to make the choice to live your best life. I've had many passions in my life, from playing pro hockey to being in the best shape of my life at 60, to running two successful businesses to being a husband, I am no stranger to taking on new and exciting endeavours. My most recent passions are public speaking and writing. I have a story to share and it's one that inspires others to live their best life.

When I was suffering in the dark and looking for help I found that there wasn't enough out there. It was a lonely place to be. I want to be the light in the dark for those like me who can't find the help they need. More of us need to share our story so that others can heal. It is through publishing and speaking that I do that. As a speaker I am engaging, transparent, honest, and informative. To find out more about booking me for your event, check out my website: glennedwards.ca

For now, I will leave you with a few questions to get you thinking about where you are at in your healing process:

1. Is there a hurt you have been holding onto that is stopping you from living your best life?

2. Do you forgive yourself for letting go of your hurt? Do you need to work on your communication skills?

3. Are you willing to do the work?

4. Are you ready to let go and live an amazing life.

Do the work!

I can help. Reach out and let's chat.

To learn more about Glenn or to connect with him about speaking at your next event, visit glennedwards.ca

Step Into Greatness

LES BROWN

You have greatness within you. You can do more than you could ever imagine. The problem most people have is that they set a goal and then ask "how can I do it? I don't have the necessary skills or education or experience".

I know what that's like. I wasted 14 years on asking myself how I could be a motivational speaker. My mind focused on the negative—on the things that were in my way, rather than on the things that were not.

It's not what you don't have but what you think you need that keeps you from getting what you want from life. But, when the dream is big enough, the obstacles don't matter. You'll get there if you stay the course. Nothing can stop you but death itself.

Think about that last statement for a minute. There's nothing on this earth that can stop you from achieving what it is that you want. So, get out of your way, and quit sabotaging your dreams. Do everything in your power to make them happen—because you cannot fail!

They say the best way to die is with your loved ones gathered around your bed. But what if you were dying and it was the ideas you never acted upon, the gifts you never used and the dreams you never pursued, that were circled around your bed? Answer that question right now. Write down your answers. If you die this very moment what ideas, what gifts, what dreams will die with you?

Then say: I refuse to die an unlived life! You beat out 40 million sperm to get here, and you'll never have to face such odds again. Walk through the field of life and leave a trail behind.

One day, one of my rich friends brought my mother a new pair of shoes for me. Now, even though we weren't well off, I didn't want them; they were a size nine and I was a size nine and a half. My mother didn't listen and told my sister to go get some Vaseline, which she rubbed all over my feet. Then my mother had me put those shoes on, minding that I didn't scrunch down the heel. She had my sister run some water in the bathtub, and I was told to get in and walk around in the water. I said that my feet hurt. She just ignored me and asked about my day at school, how everything went and did I get into any fights? I knew what she was up to, that she was trying to distract me, so I said I had only gotten into three fights. After a while mother asked me if my feet still hurt. I admitted that the pain had indeed lessened. She kept me walking in that tub until I had a brand new pair of comfortable, size nine and a half shoes.

You see, once the leather in the shoes got wet, they stretched! And what you need to do is stretch a little. I believe that most people don't set high goals and miss them, but rather, they set lower goals and hit them and then they stay there, stuck on the side of the highway of life. When you're pursuing your greatness, you don't know what your limitations are, and you need to act like you don't have any. If you shoot for the moon and miss, you'll still be in the stars.

You also need coaching (a mentor). Why? There are times you, too, will find yourself parked on the side of the highway of life with no gas in the vehicle. What you need then is someone to stop and offer to pick up some gas down the road a ways and bring it back to you. That person is your coach. Yes, they are there for advice, but their main job is to help you through the difficulties that life throws at all of us.

Another reason for having a coach is that you can't see the picture when you're in the frame. In other words, he or she can often see where you are with a clarity and focus that's unavailable to you. They're not going to leave you parked along the road of life, nor are they going to allow you to be stuck in the moment like a photo in a frame.

And let's say you just can't see your way forward. You don't believe it's possible. Sometimes you just have to believe in someone's belief in you. This could be your coach, a loved one or even a staunch friend. You need to hear them say you can do it, time and again. Because, after all, faith comes from hearing and hearing and hearing.

Look at it this way. Most people fail because of possibility blindness. They can't see what lies before them. There are always possibilities. Because of this, your dream is possible. You may fail often. In fact, I want you to say this: I will fail my way to success. Here is why.

I had a TV show that failed. I felt I had to go back to public speaking. I had failed, so I parked my car for ten years. Then I saw Dr. Wayne Dyer was still on PBS and I decided to call them. They said they would love to work with me and asked where I had been. I wasn't as good as I had been ten years before, as I was out of practice, but I still had to get back in the game. I was determined to drive on empty.

Listen to recordings, go to seminars, challenge yourself, and you'll begin to step into your greatness, you'll begin to fill yourself with the energy you need to climb to greater heights. Most people never attend a seminar. They won't invest money in books or audio programs. You put yourself in the top 5 percent just by making a different choice than the average person. This is called contrary thinking. It's a concept taken from the financial industry. One considers choosing the exact opposite behaviour of the average person as a way to get better than average results. You don't have to make the contrarian choice, but if you don't have anything to lose by going that road, why not consider the option?

Make your move before you're ready. Walk by faith not by sight and make sure you're happy doing it. If you can't be happy, what else is there? Helen Keller said, "Life is short, eat the dessert first."

What is faith? Many of us think of God when we think of faith. A different viewpoint claims that faith is a firm belief in something for which there is no proof. I would rather think of faith as something that is believed especially with strong conviction. It is this last definition I am referring to when I say walk by faith not by sight. Be happy and go forth with strong conviction that you are destined for greatness.

An important step on your way to greatness is to take the time to detoxify. You've got to look at the people in your life. What are they doing for you? Are they setting a pace that you can follow? If not, whose pace have you adjusted to? If you're the smartest in your group, find a new group.

Are the people in your life pulling you down or lifting you up? You know what to do, right? Banish the negative and stay with the positive; it's that simple. Dr. Norman Vincent Peale once said (when I was in the audience), "You are special. You have greatness within you, and you can do more than you could ever possibly imagine."

He overrode the inner conversations in my mind and reached the heart of me. He set me on fire. This is yet another reason for seeking out the help of a coach or mentor or other new people in your life. They can do what Dr. Peale did for me. They can set your passion free.

How important is it to have the right kind of person/people on your side? There was a study done that determined it takes 16 people saying you can do something to overcome one person who says you can't do something. That's right, one negative, unsupportive person can wipe out the work of 16 other supportive people. The message can't be any clearer than that.

Let's face the cold, hard truth: most people stay in park along the highway of life. They never feel the passion, the love for their fellow man, or for the work they do. They are stuck in the proverbial rut. What's the reason? There are many reasons, but only one common factor: fear — fear of change, fear of failure, fear of success, fear they may not be good enough, fear of competition, even fear of rejection.

"Rejection is a myth," says Jack Canfield, co-author of The Chicken Soup for the Soul series. "It's not like you get a slap in the face each time you are rejected." Why not take every "no" you receive as a vitamin, and every time you take one know you are another step closer to success.

You will win if you don't quit. Even a broken clock is right twice a day.

Professional baseball players, on average, get on base just three times out of every ten times they face the opposing pitcher. Even superstars fail half of the time they appear at the plate.

Top commissioned salespeople face similar odds. They may make one sale from every three people they see, but it will have taken them between 75 and 100 telephone calls to make the 15 appointments they need to close their five sales for the week. And these are statistics for the elite. Most salespeople never reach these kinds of numbers.

People don't spend their lives working for just one company anymore. This means you must build up a set of skills and experiences that are portable. This can be done a number of ways, but my favourite approaches follow.

You must be willing to do the things others won't do in order to have tomorrow the things that others don't have. Provide more service than you get paid for. Set some high standards for yourself.

Begin each day with your most difficult task. The rest of the day will seem more enjoyable and a whole lot easier.

Someone needs help with a problem? Be the solution to that problem.

Also, find those tasks that are being consistently ignored and do them. You'll be surprised by the results. An acquaintance of mine used this approach at a number of entry-level positions and each time he quickly ended up being offered a position in management.

You must increase your energy. Kick it up a notch. We are spirits having a physical existence; let your spirit shine. Quit frittering away your energy. Use it to move you closer to the achievement of your dreams. Refuse to spend it on non-productive activities.

What do people say about you when you leave a room? Are you willing to take responsibility—to walk your talk. There is a terrible epidemic sweeping our nation, and it is the refusal to take responsibility for one's actions. Consider that at some point in any situation there will have been a moment where you could have done something to change the outcome. To that end you are responsible for what happened. It's a hard thing to accept, but it's true.

Life's hard. It was hard when I was told I had cancer. I had sunken into despair, and was hiding away in my study when my son came in. My son asked me if I was going to die. What could I do? I told him I was going to fight, even though I was scared. I also told him that I needed some help. Not because I was weak but because I wanted to stay strong. Keep asking until you get help. Don't stop until you get it.

A setback is the setup for a comeback. A setback is simply a misstep on the long road of success. It means nothing in the larger scheme of things. And, surprisingly, it sets you up for your next win. It tends to focus you and your energy on your immediate goals, paving the way for your next sprint, for your comeback.

It's worth it. Your dreams are worth the sacrifices you'll have to make to achieve them. Find five reasons that will make your dreams worth it for you. Say to yourself, I refuse to live an unlived life.

If you are casual about your dreams, you'll end up a casualty. You must be passionate about your dreams, living and breathing them throughout your days. You've got to be hungry! People who are hungry refuse to take no for an answer. Make NO your vitamin. Be unstoppable. Be hungry.

Let me give you an example of what I mean by hungry …

I decided I wanted to become a disc jockey, so I went down to the local radio station and asked the manager, Mr. Milton "Butterball" Smith, if he had a job available for a disc jockey. He said he did not. The next day I went back, and Mr. Smith asked "Weren't you here yesterday?" I explained that I was just checking to see if anyone was sick or had died. He responded by telling me not to come back again. Day three, I went back again—with the same story. Mr. Smith told me to get out of there. I came back the fourth day and gave Mr. Smith my story one more time. He was so beside himself that he told me to get him a cup of coffee. I said, "Yes, sir!" That's how I became the errand boy.

While working as an errand boy at the station, I took every opportunity to hang out with the deejays and to observe them working. After I had taught myself how to run the control room, it was just a matter of biding my time.

Then one day an opportunity presented itself. One of the disc jockeys by the name of Rockin' Roger was drinking heavily while he was on the air. It was a Saturday afternoon. And there I was, the only one there.

I watched him through the control-room window. I walked back and forth in front of that window like a cat watching a mouse, saying "Drink, Rock, Drink!" I was young. I was ready. And I was hungry.

Pretty soon, the phone rang. It was the station manager. He said, "Les, this is Mr. Klein."

I said, "Yes, I know."

He said, "Rock can't finish his program."

I said, "Yes sir, I know."

He said, "Would you call one of the other disc jockeys to fill in?"

I said, "Yes sir, I sure will, sir."

And when he hung up, I said, "Now he must think I'm crazy." I called up my mama and my girlfriend, Cassandra, and I told them, "Ya'll go out on the front porch and turn up the radio, I'M ABOUT TO COME ON THE AIR!"

I waited 15 or 20 minutes and called the station manager back. I said, "Mr. Klein, I can't find NOBODY!"

He said, "Young boy, do you know how to work the controls?"

I said, "Yes, sir."

He said, "Go in there, but don't say anything. Hear me?"

I said, "Yes, sir."

I couldn't wait to get old Rock out of the way. I went in there, took my seat behind that turntable, flipped on the microphone and let 'er rip.

"Look out, this is me, LB., triple P. Les Brown your platter-playin' papa. There were none before me and there will be none after me, therefore that makes me the one and only. Young and single and love to mingle, certified, bona fide and indubitably qualified to bring you satisfaction and a whole lot of action. Look out baby, I'm your LOVE man."

I WAS HUNGRY!

During my adult life I've been a deejay, a radio station manager, a Democrat in the Ohio Legislature, a minister, a TV personality, an author and a public speaker, but I've always looked after what I valued most—my mother. What I want for her is one of my dreams, one of my goals.

My life has been a true testament to the power of positive thinking and the infinite human potential. I was born in an abandoned building on a floor in Liberty City, a low-income section of Miami, Florida, and adopted at six weeks of age by Mrs. Mamie Brown, a 38-year-old single woman, cafeteria cook and domestic worker. She had very little education or financial means, but a very big heart and the desire to care for myself and my twin brother. I call myself Mrs. Mamie Brown's Baby Boy and I say that all that I am and all that I ever hoped to be, I owe to my mother.

My determination and persistence in searching for ways to help my mother overcome poverty and developing my philosophy to do whatever it takes to achieve success led me to become a distinguished authority on harnessing human potential and success. That philosophy is best expressed by the following …

"If you want a thing bad enough to go out and fight for it,
to work day and night for it,
to give up your time, your peace and your sleep for it…
if all that you dream and scheme is about it,
and life seems useless and worthless without it…
if you gladly sweat for it and fret for it and plan for it
and lose all your terror of the opposition for it…
if you simply go after that thing you want
with all of your capacity, strength and sagacity,
faith, hope and confidence and stern pertinacity…
if neither cold, poverty, famine, nor gout,
sickness nor pain, of body and brain,
can keep you away from the thing that you want…
if dogged and grim you beseech and beset it,
with the help of God, you will get it!"

Branding
Small Business

RAYMOND AARON

B randing is an incredibly important tool for creating and building your business. Large companies have been benefiting from branding ever since people first started selling things to other people. Branding made those businesses big.

If you're a small business owner, you probably imagine that small companies are different and don't need branding as much as large companies do. Not true. The truth is small businesses need branding just as much, if not more, than large companies.

Perhaps you've thought about branding, but assumed you'd need millions of dollars to do it properly, or that branding is just the same thing as marketing. Nothing could be further from the truth.

Marketing is the engine of your company's success. Branding is the fuel in that engine.

In the old days, salespeople were a big part of the selling process. They recommended one product over another and laid out the reasons why it was better. Salespeople had credibility because they knew about all the products, and customers often took the advice they had to offer.

Today, consumers control the buying process. They shop in big box stores, super-sized supermarkets, and over the Internet — where there are no salespeople. Buyers now get online and gather information beforehand. They learn about all the products available and look to see if there really is any difference between them. Consumers also read reviews and check social media to see if both the company and the product are reputable. In other words, they want to know what the brand is all about.

The way of commerce used to be: "Nothing happens till something is sold." Today it's: "Nothing happens till something is branded!"

DEFINING A BRAND

A brand is a proper name that stands for something. It lives in the consumer's mind, has positive or negative characteristics, and invokes a feeling or an image. In short, it's a person's perception of a product or a company.

When all goes well, consumers associate the same characteristics with a brand that the company talks about in its advertising, public relations, marketing and sales materials. Of course, when a product doesn't live up to what the company says about it, the brand gets a bad reputation. On the other hand, if a product or service over-delivers on the promises made, the brand can become a superstar.

RECOGNIZING BRANDING AND ITS CHARACTERISTICS

Branding is the science and art of making something that isn't unique, unique. Branding in the marketplace is the same as branding on a ranch. On a ranch, ranchers use branding to differentiate their cattle from every other rancher's cattle (because all cattle look pretty much the same). In the marketplace, branding is what makes a product stand out in a crowd of similar products. The right branding gets you noticed, remembered and sold — or perhaps I should say bought, because today it is all about buying, not selling.

There are four main characteristics of branding that make it an integral part of the marketing and purchasing process.

1. Branding makes you trustworthy and known

Branding makes a product more special than other products. With branding, a normal, everyday product has a personality, and a first and last name, and people know who you are.

In today's marketplace, most products are, more or less, just like their competition. Toilet paper is toilet paper, milk is milk, and a grocery store by any other name is still a grocery store. However, branding takes a product and makes it unique. For example, high-quality drinking water is available from just about every tap in the Western world and it's free, but people pay good money for it when it comes in a bottle. Branding takes bottled water and makes Evian.

Furthermore, every aspect of your brand gives potential customers a feeling or comfort level that they associate with you. The more powerful and positive that feeling is, the more easily and more frequently they will want to do business with you and, indeed, will do business with you.

2. Branding differentiates you from others

Strong branding makes you better than your competition, and makes your product name memorable and easy to remember. Even if your product is absolutely the same as every other product like it, branding makes it special. Branding makes it the first product a consumer thinks about when deciding to make a purchase.

Branding also makes a product seem popular. Everyone knows about it, which implicitly says people like it. And, if people like it, it must be good.

3. Branding makes you worth more money

The stronger your branding is, the more likely people are willing to spend that little bit extra because they believe you, your product, your service, or your business are worth it. They may say they won't, but they will. They do it all the time.

For example, a one-pound box of Godiva chocolates costs about $40; the same weight of Hershey's Kisses costs about $4. The quality of the chocolate isn't ten times greater. The reason people buy Godiva is that the brand Godiva means "gift" whereas the brand Hershey means "snack". Gifts obviously cost more than snacks.

4. Branding pre-sells your product

In the buying age, people most often make the decision on which products to pick up before they walk into the store. The stronger the branding, the more likely people are to think in terms of your product rather than the product category. For example, people are as likely, maybe even more likely, to add Hellmann's to the shopping list as they are to write down simply mayo. The same is true for soda, ketchup, and many other products with successful, strong branding.

Plus, as soon as a shopper gets to the shelf, branding can provide a quick reminder of what products to grab in a few ways:

- An icon or logo
- A specific color
- An audio icon

BRANDING IN A SMALL BUSINESS

Big companies spend millions of dollars on advertising, marketing, and public relations (PR) to build recognition of a new product name. They get their selling messages out to the public using television, radio, magazines, and the Internet. They can even throw money at damage control when necessary. The strategies for branding are the same in a small business, but the scale, costs, and a few of the tactics change.

Make your brand name work harder

The name of a small business can mean everything in terms of branding. Your brand name needs to work harder for your business than you do. It's the first thing a prospective customer sees, and it is how they will remember you. A brand name has to be memorable when spoken, and focused in its meaning. If the name doesn't represent what consumers believe about a product and the company that makes it, then that brand will fail.

In building your product's reputation and image, less is often significantly more. Make sure the name you choose immediately gives a sense of what you do.

Large corporations have millions of dollars to take a meaningless brand name and make it stand for something. Small businesses don't, so use words that really mean something. Strive for something interesting and be right on point. You don't need to be boring.

Plumbers, for example, would do well setting themselves apart with names like "The On-Time Plumber" or "24/7 Plumbing". The same is true for electricians, IT providers, or even marketing consultants. Plenty of other types of business are so general in nature they just don't work hard enough in a business or product name.

Even the playing field: The Net

The Internet has leveled the playing field for small businesses like nothing else. You can use the Internet in several ways to market your brand:

Website: Developing and maintaining a website is easier than ever. Anyone can find your business regardless of its size.

Social Media: Facebook and Twitter can promote your brand in a cost-effective manner.

BUILDING YOUR BRAND WITH THE BRANDING LADDER

Even if you do everything perfectly the first time (and I don't know anyone who does), branding takes time. How much time isn't just up to you, but you can speed things along by understanding the different levels of branding, as well as the business and marketing strategies that can get you to the top.

Introducing the Branding Ladder

Moving through the levels of branding is like climbing a ladder to the top of the marketplace. The Branding Ladder has five distinct rungs and, unlike stairs, you can't take them two at a time. You have to take them in order, and some businesses spend more time on each rung than others.

You can also think of the Branding Ladder in terms of a scale from zero to ten. Everyone starts at zero. If you properly climb the ladder, you can end up at 12 out of 10. The Branding Ladder below shows a special rung at the top of the ladder that can take your business over the top. The following section explains the Branding Ladder and how your small business can move up it.

THE BRANDING LADDER	
Brand Advocacy	**12/10**
Brand Insistence	**10/10**
Brand Preference	**3/10**
Brand Awareness	**1/10**
Brand Absence	**0/10**

Rung 1: Living in the void

Your business, in fact every business, starts at the bottom rung, which is called brand absence, meaning you have no brand whatsoever except your own name. On a scale of one to ten, brand absence is, of course, zero. That's the worst place to live and obviously the most difficult entrepreneurially. The good news is that the only way is up.

Ninety-seven percent of businesses live on this rung of the Branding Ladder. They earn far less than they want to earn, far less than they should earn, and far less than they would earn if they did exactly the same work under a real brand.

Rung 2: Achieving awareness

Brand awareness is a good first step up the ladder to the second rung. Actually, it's really good, especially because 97 percent of businesses never get there. You want people to be aware of you. When person A speaks to person B and says, "Have you heard of "The 24/7 Plumber?" You want the answer to be "yes".

On that scale of one to ten, however, brand awareness is only a one. It's better than nothing, but not that much better. Although people know of your brand, being aware doesn't mean that they are interested in buying it. Coca Cola drinkers know about Pepsi, but they don't drink it.

Rung 3: Becoming the preferred brand

Getting to the third rung, brand preference, is definitely a real step up. This rung means that people prefer to use your product or service rather than that of your competition. They believe there is a real difference between you and others, and you're their first choice. This rung is a crucial branding stage for parity products, such as bottled water and breakfast cereals, not to mention plumbers, electricians, lawyers, and all the others. Brand preference is clearly better than brand awareness, but it's less than halfway up the ladder.

Car rental companies represent a perfect example of why brand preference may not be enough. When someone lands at an airport and needs to rent a car on the spot, he or she may go straight to the preferred rental counter. If that company has a car available, it's a sale. However, if all the cars for that company have been rented, the person will move to the next rental kiosk without much thought, because one rental car is just as good as another.

Exerting Brand Preference needs to be easy and convenient

If all you have is brand preference, your business is on shaky ground and you can lose business for the feeblest of reasons. Very few people go to a second or third supermarket just to find their favorite brand of bottled water. Similarly, a shopper may prefer one store over another but, if both stores sell the same products, he or she will often go to the closest store even if it is not the better liked one. The reason for staying nearby does not need to be a dramatic one — the shopper may simply be tired, on a tight schedule, or not in the mood to travel.

Rung 4: Making it you and only you

When your customers are so committed to your product or service that they won't accept a substitute, you have reached the fourth rung of the Branding Ladder. All companies strive to reach this place, called brand insistence.

Brand insistence means that someone's experience with a product in terms of performance, durability, customer service, and image has been sufficiently exceptional. As a result, the product has earned an incredible level of loyalty. If the product isn't available where the customer is, he or she will literally not buy something else. Rather, the person will look for the preferred product elsewhere. Can you imagine what a fabulous place this is for a company to be? Brand insistence is the best of the best, the perfect ten out of ten, the whole ball of wax.

Apple is a perfect example of brand insistence

Apple users don't just think, they know in their heads and hearts, that anything made by Apple is technologically-advanced, user-friendly, and just all-around superior. Committed to everything Apple, Mac users won't even entertain the thought that a PC may have positive attributes.

Apple people love everything about their Macs, iPads, iPhones, the Mac stores and all those apps. When the company introduces a new product, many of its brand-insistent fans actually wait in line overnight to be one of the first to have it. Steve Jobs is one of their idols.

Considering one big potential problem

Unfortunately, you can lose brand insistence much more quickly than you can achieve it. Brand-insistent customers have such high expectations that they can be disillusioned or disappointed by just one bad product experience. You also have to consistently reinforce the positives because insistence can fade over time. Even someone who has bought and re-bought a specific brand of car for the last 20 years can decide it's just time for a change. That's how fickle the world is.

At ten out of ten, brand insistence may seem like the top rung of the ladder, but it's not. One rung is actually better, and it involves getting your brand-insistent customers to keep polishing your brand for you.

Rung 5: Getting customers to do the work for you

Brand advocacy is the highest rung on the ladder. It's better than ten out of ten because you have customers who are so happy with your product that they want everyone to know about it and use it. Think of them as uber-fans. Not only do they recommend you to friends and family, they also practically shout your praises from the rooftops, interrupt conversations among strangers to give their opinion, and tell everyone they meet how fantastic you are. Most companies can only aspire to this level of customer satisfaction. Apple is one of the few large corporations in recent history that has brand advocates all over the world.

- Brand advocacy does the following five extraordinary things for your company. Brand advocacy:

- Provides a level of visibility that you couldn't pay for if you tried. Brand advocates are so enthusiastic they talk about you all the time, and reach people in ways general media and public relations can't. You get great visibility because they make sure people actually listen.

- Delivers free advertising and public relations. Companies love the extra super-positive messaging, all for free.

- Affords a level of credibility that literally can't be bought. Brand advocates are more than just walking testimonials. They are living proof that you are the best.

- Provides pre-sold prospective customers. Advocate recommendations carry so much weight that they are worth much more than plain referrals. They deliver customers ready and committed to purchasing your product or service.

- Increases profits exponentially. Brand advocates are money-making machines for your business because they increase sales and decrease marketing costs.

For these reasons, brand advocacy is 12 out of 10!!

BRANDING YOURSELF: HOW TO DO SO IN FOUR EASY WAYS

If you're interested in branding your product or company, you may not be sure where to begin. The good news: I'm here to help. You can brand in many ways, but here I pare it down to four ways to help you start:

Branding by association

This way involves hanging out with and being seen with people who are very much higher than you in your particular niche.

Branding by achievement

This way repurposes your previous achievements.

Branding by testimonial

This way makes use of the testimonials that you receive but have likely never used.

Branding by WOW

A WOW is the pleasantly unexpected, the equivalent of going the extra mile. The easiest and most certain way to WOW people is to tell them that you've written a book. To discover how you can write a book, go to www.BrandingSmallBusinessForDummies.com.

Sex, Love and Relationships

DR. JOHN GRAY

J ust as great sex is important to lasting love, good health is important to sex and relationships. About 12 years ago, I cured myself of early stage Parkinson's disease. The doctors were amazed, but my wife was even more amazed. She noted that our relationship and sex life had become dramatically better. It turns out that the natural supplements I used to reverse Parkinson's can also make you more attentive and loving in your relationship. At that point, I realized that good relationship skills alone were not enough to sustain love and passion for a lifetime.

I shared many insights gained from my 40 years' experience as a marriage counselor and coach in *Men Are From Mars, Women Are From Venus*. And while my insights go a long way towards helping men and women understand and support each other, good communication skills alone are not always enough. For better relationships, we not only need to be healthy, but we must also experience optimum brain function.

If you are tired, depressed, anxious, not sleeping well, or in pain, then certainly romantic feelings will become a thing of the past. My recovery from Parkinson's revealed to me the profound connection between the quality of our health and our relationships. This insight has motivated me, over the past twelve years, to research the secrets of optimum health as a foundation for lasting love.

These are health secrets that are generally not explored in medical school. In medical school, doctors are indoctrinated into the culture of examining the symptoms, identifying the sickness, and prescribing a drug to treat that sickness. They learn very little about how to be healthy or to sustain successful relationships.

There are no university courses entitled "Better Nutrition For Better Sex". Drugs sometimes save lives, but they also have negative side effects that do little to preserve the passion in a relationship. Ideally, drugs should be used as a last resort and 90 % of our health plan should be drug free. From this perspective, the heath care crisis, as well as our high rate of divorce in America, is indirectly caused by our dependence on doctors and prescription drugs.

Most people have not even considered that taking prescribed drugs (even for the small stuff) can weaken their relationships, which in turn makes them more vulnerable to more disease. For example, if you are feeling depressed or anxious, a drug may numb your pain, but it does nothing to help you correct the cause of your problem. It can even prevent you from feeling your natural motivation to get the emotional support you need. In a variety of ways, our common health complaints are all expressions of two major conditions: our lack of education to identify and support unmet gender-specific emotional needs; and our lack of education to identify and support unmet gender-specific nutritional needs.

With an understanding of natural solutions that have been around for thousands of years, drugs are not needed to treat many common complaints. Some symptoms like low energy, weight gain, allergies, hormonal imbalance, mood swings, poor sleep, indigestion, lack of focus, ADD and ADHD, procrastination, low motivation, memory loss, decreased libido, PMS, vaginal dryness, muscle and joint pain, or the lack of passion in life and/or our relationships can be treated drug-free. By using drugs (even over-the-counter drugs) to treat these common complaints, our bodies and relationships are weakened, making us more vulnerable to bigger and more costly health challenges like cancer, diabetes, heart disease, auto-immune disease, dementia, and Alzheimer's. In simple terms, by handling the easy stuff (the common complaints) without doctors and drugs, we can protect ourselves from the big stuff (cancer, heart disease, dementia, etc.) We can be healthy and also enjoy lasting love and passion in our personal lives.

Even if you are taking anti-depressants or hormone replacement therapy, sometimes all it takes to stop treating the symptom is to directly handle the cause. With specific mineral orotates (something most people have never heard of) or omega three oil from the brains of salmon, your stress levels immediately drop and you begin to feel happy and in love again.

For every health challenge, we have explored the effects on our relationships, with as well as natural remedies that can sometimes produce immediate positive results. You can find these natural solutions to common health complaints for free at my website: www.MarsVenus.com.

What they don't teach in medical school is how to be healthy and happy without the use of drugs or hormone replacement. By refusing drugs and taking responsibility for your health, a wealth of new possibilities can become available to you. We are designed to be healthy and happy, and it is within our reach if we commit to increasing our knowledge.

New research regarding the brain differences in men and women reveals how specific nutritional supplements, combined with gender-specific relationship and self-nurturing skills, can stimulate the hormones of health, happiness and increased energy. Over the past 10 years in my healing center in California, I witnessed how natural solutions coupled with gender-specific relationship skills could solve our common health complaints without drugs. By addressing these common complaints without prescribed drugs, not only do we feel better, but our relationships have the potential to improve dramatically.

Ultimately the cause of all our common complaints is higher stress levels. Researchers around the world all agree that chronic stress levels in our bodies provide a basis for any and all disease to take hold. An easy and quick solution for lowering our stress reactions is specific nutritional support combined with gender-smart relationship skills. Extra nutritional support is needed because stress depletes the body very quickly of essential nutrients. When a car engine is running more quickly, it uses fuel more quickly. When we are stressed, we need both extra nutrients and extra emotional support. Understanding what we need to take and where to get it requires education. Every week day at www.MarsVenus.com I have a live daily show where I freely answer questions and provide this much-needed new gender-specific insight.

At www.MarsVenus.com, we are happy to share what we have learned for creating healthy bodies and positive relationships. You can find a host of natural solutions for common complaints and feel confident that you have the power to feel fully alive with an abundance of energy and positive feelings that will enrich all your relationships.

for creating useful bodies and . . .

Perspective Thinking

ANDREA NGUI

O ur experiences shape our perspectives. Yet, our perspectives also shape our experiences. It is a continual circle. Throughout my journey, I learned how shifting my perspective altered my experiences and opened the door to some amazing opportunities. Let me share my journey with you, as well as how shifting your perspective can help you change your life.

Often, the choices you make come down to your perspective and how it impacts your thinking. As an entrepreneur, I love the idea of breaking out of the status quo to create an amazing life. Taking that step to break my own status quo set me up to experience things and places I hadn't thought possible.

To me, the status quo is defined as settling for a corporate job, one where you spend your time making money for someone else. I have always wanted to be my own boss, but that dream had to be put on hold as I started working and gaining experience in various roles, including retail, restaurants, geographic information systems, and sales. I hopped jobs based on the money, but more importantly, I gained a lot of experience in many roles and won several awards. I focused on the material benefits, even though I wasn't focused on what type of career spoke to me.

Eventually, I realized there was more to my career than just making money. So, I asked myself what I wanted to do with the rest of my professional life.

Perhaps you have faced this situation in your own life. You know what you don't want to be doing with your career, but you haven't zeroed in on what you do want. Part of my early journey to break the status quo was understanding how my perspective influenced my thinking and my choices. I wasn't listening to my gut feelings or following my intuition. The result was that I allowed my thinking to be dominated by fears or the almighty dollar, instead of chasing my dreams. My perspective had been narrowed by the status quo that I was mindlessly following.

Things had to change as I faced some life-threatening challenges. To create the drastic change in my lifestyle, I had to start taking my health and happiness more seriously than I ever had before. One of the major challenges I live with is being seriously allergic to certain foods. I have dealt with multiple anaphylactic episodes, which meant that various jobs could expose me to life-threatening situations in a matter of moments. I needed to create a safer external environment to live in. Coping with my allergies to food isn't easy. I might as well live in bubble wrap. I could live in fear and keep myself from exploring new places and new experiences in an attempt to protect myself from everything that can harm me. It also made me realize that life can be over faster than expected. I decided to shift gears in figuring out how to start living my dream lifestyle, i.e. what makes me happy and healthy. This meant I had to gain clarity in my professional life.

Another major factor that I had to confront was chronic pain. I simply pushed myself more every day with what had to be done. I pushed my tolerance limits to the max, which meant I jeopardized my health and wellbeing. Shifting my perspective meant changing my approach. I had to figure out how to stop being overly focused on the future and, rather, focused on enjoying the present. Instead of pushing at full speed physically, I took time to relax by watching movies and listening to music. A benefit of taking this time for myself was that it also inspired my creativity.

Since so much of what I wanted was wrapped up in my health, I concentrated on that first and foremost. I visited many health practitioners, doctors, neurological clinic, conducted a CAT scan and MRI. All my results concluded my nervous system is functioning perfectly healthy. Nothing made sense. My body was constantly in pain. It was painful resting, walking, putting clothes on hangers, to swimming in the water. I found a network spinal analysis (NSA) chiropractor and increasing my physical fitness made the chronic pain permanently disappear. My chronic pain stemmed from life stressors.

I also started exercising to improve my physical endurance. Soon, I signed myself up for my first 5k and 10k road races. The benefits were not limited to physical ones. Those endorphins and the sense of accomplishment after each race spurred me to keep up my efforts.

I have also found that slowing down to take more time for self-care allows me to think with clarity. With a humbler and steadier attitude, I am no longer watching life bypass me, but instead I am enjoying life to the fullest. I am living my best lifestyle today, not later, because later may never come.

SETTING GOALS AS PART OF THE SHIFT

One of the benefits of opening my mind and heart to perspective thinking is that I listen more spiritually to the universe, using its guidance to unfold my life.

Your perspective can make you feel as if you do not have control over what is happening in your life. Professionally, you can feel as if you are a hamster on a wheel, trapped in your personal status quo. Shifting your perspective can be challenging if you are not sure what direction you truly want to go. I was so busy chasing money that I wasn't focused on achieving the right career for myself. Once I stopped dreaming and started to take action in defining my life goals and the lifestyle I wanted to live, I came to the realization of what my life profession would become.

If you meet people who have achieved their life goals and created their ideal life, they all talk about the fact that they took action. They moved! Life goals are going to set the framework for your actions and choices. Recognize that your perspective throughout life is key to staying on track to achieve what you truly desire in life.

Life is going to throw curve balls and readjusting is a necessary part of reaching your life goals. Taking the time to move at a slower pace by allocating time and space to learn from and reflect on what you have already accomplished will help you continue setting milestones that get you closer to your goals.

Identifying your life goals means that you can start laying out a timeline with milestones to help you reach your goals. Take notice of the fact that you can plan milestones forever, but if you don't start moving and take that first step, then it will just remain a to-do list with nothing crossed off and accomplished.

Start with a smaller goal, just to get moving. After all, once you achieve that first small goal, it can be all the motivation you need to tackle the next one and build resilience and consistency as you encounter setbacks. The beauty of these small steps is that even with setbacks, what you already accomplished can give you the strength, inspiration, and courage to keep moving forward. Now let's talk about some of those setbacks or obstacles, especially those that you create within yourself.

IDENTIFYING OBSTACLES TO SHIFT YOUR PERSPECTIVE

It is so easy to point the finger at your circumstances and the individuals around you as the reasons why you cannot move forward. You create reasons why you can't do something or why it is impossible. You may even blame others for your inability to accomplish your goals. The point is that those excuses and the blaming of others allows you to stay still and feel comfortable with not creating permanent change in your life. We've all heard the saying "Try, try, try again, and never give up." Perhaps giving up on your current direction by turning around into a new direction may just give you that zest feeling you long for in life. Moving forward isn't a straight line. In sports, players keep moving forward, but not always in a straight line, to get another touchdown, a basket, or a homerun.

Ask yourself, is it circumstances or an excuse that I am telling myself? Too often, our excuses block us from seeing the solutions that could be right in front of us. You need to get out of your own way. When you make excuses, you are creating barriers to dictate which way you should live.

Let's face it, self-inflicted fearmongering can be a big form of self-sabotage.

You can build up the fears in your mind to the point that you choose inaction instead of moving forward with courage.

Negative thinking can be encouraged or discouraged, depending on the thoughts you allow to be planted in your mind. You might feel like you are getting ahead, but the truth is that you are not really getting anywhere. Instead, you are simply stuck doing what you did yesterday, and if anyone points out to you that fact, then you have excuses for why you aren't progressing. You treat challenges as obstacles that cannot be overcome.

For instance, if you're dealing with a chronic health condition, you may have a tougher battle against negative thinking. After all, you are likely dealing with a variety of challenges, such as pain or limited range of motion. The physical limitations can be even harder to deal with if it impacts your independence. You can become exhausted, mentally and physically. Building a strong, healthier mindset will help you cope and potentially overcome your chronic health issue.

On the flip side, you can be the source of negative thinking for others and end up causing toxicity in someone else's thoughts. If you find yourself surrounded by those who talk negatively, stop for a moment and analyze how you are speaking. Are you drawing negativity to yourself? Shifting your perspective means being honest with yourself about the thoughts and words you allow yourself to use to describe yourself and others.

Part of changing or shifting your perspective involves power shifting your thoughts to lessen the impact of negative thinking. Once you start shifting your thinking, you will notice a breakthrough in defeating excuses and self-sabotage.

Another way to stop your negative thinking is to look at what you are feeding your brain in terms of social media. After all, there are arguments and differences of opinion that play out over the internet. You might have been in a good mood, but then you read something online and became instantly angry, even though nothing happened to you personally.

Have you ever been in a performance sports car? As the driver pushes on the gas pedal, the car can accelerate over 60 miles per hour in less than two seconds. Visualize your life performing like a sports car. If you don't push the gas pedal and tap into your power, then it is not going to perform like you anticipated. Constantly shifting your perspective as quickly as the speed of a performance sports car is key to learning what it takes to live a successful life.

Here is the important thing to remember before you can make any changes in your life. When changing your mindset, start with the invisible internal dialogue. This needs to occur before the visible external changes can properly manifest. The results of your thinking will be shown through your actions and decisions.

Your inner voice can often be one of the greatest challenges that you need to overcome to create change in your life. If you focus on thoughts based on fear, then you are going to end up becoming your own blockade. Your fear will constantly dictate what you do, trapping you in a place where you feel that everything around you is a huge risk. You could be living a fun and enjoyable life. All you need to do is conquer your fears. Always move forward with courage, even if you still feel the fear within you.

For instance, you might not like the life you are living, but it is the only one that you know. Fear might make you resist change, simply because you fear that you have so much to lose if you change. So why should you bother to make the effort? Essentially, you are self-defeating, even before you have tried or given change a chance.

Here is the reality that we all have to face. Change is coming regardless of whether we want it or not. While change can equate with loss or challenges, there is also much that can be gained.

Take a minute and look at a situation where you are fearful of change and losing what you have. Now, instead of focusing on what you might lose, let's shift to thinking about all that you might gain.

Instead of waiting for the world to bring joy and happiness into your world, start thinking about how you can create it on your own. This may include changing your routine or making a giant leap of change in your job or living situation. There are so many stories out there of individuals deciding to take a giant leap. Their experiences show how changing your thinking can allow you to make some amazing leaps in life. Your thinking can inspire you to act and make choices that align with the life you desire to live.

You need to figure out what type of life you want to live. Start focusing on what brings you joy. Often, it can be hard to separate the life that you want from the life that you are expected to live by society and your family. If you shape your life around the expectations of others, even your loved ones, then you are essentially disowning your true self for an imitation. Now, the process of letting go of those expectations and claiming the life you want to live does take effort.

How many times have you been in the position where you tried to do something and then tanked, such as a road race? Instead of crossing the finish line victoriously, you fell and twisted an ankle just a few feet past the starting line. Your perception of that experience can go one of two ways.

The first way is that you can look at that race and decide you will never run again. The second way is to look at that race and make a decision that you are going to learn from that experience. Perhaps you need different shoes, or another training regimen.

Notice that the second perspective was about finding the ways that you can learn from the experience, improve, and have a successful outcome the next time. That is a perspective that embraces learning, change, and growth. Training and practice are part of the journey.

To get to where you want to be, you need to have a clear vision of what type of life you want. Once you know where you want to be at a certain point, then you need to create an action plan around getting from point A to point B. When you create your action plan, it has to be wrapped around your perspective that it is possible to achieve.

Here is a quick exercise. Ask yourself what you tolerate from yourself that you might not tolerate in others and write it down. Remember, when you make an excuse, you are not holding yourself accountable in being true to yourself. How would you feel if you discarded things you tolerated? How would your life change?

You have to listen to your gut feelings. When you smother intuition, inertia kicks in and you get stuck with your decision making. Spend time to gain clarity with your mind to let yourself properly receive the message from your intuition.

When I was stuck in my status quo, doing the job and exhausting myself in the process, I realized that no one was going to be as concerned about my pursuit of happiness in living out my dream lifestyle than me.

No one is truly stopping you or standing in your way. The only person doing that is you! Recognize that other people will never truly understand what you need to do until you take action and they start to see the results.

Then they will understand more in-depth what you need to do and why you need to do it. Who knows? You might end up inspiring them to shift their own perspective and start creating something amazing in their own lives.

It is about designing the life you want to live. Acknowledge you deserve to live an amazing life. Become the leader of your own life destiny. Be your own hero and a role model to others.

Once I focused on creating that lifestyle which I had designed for myself, then I started to live the best years of my life. The radiant self-fulfilling lifestyle journey that I began creating for myself has been the most wonderful and marvelous experience, and I get to experience it every single day. The amount of peace and harmony that I know is so abundant. It motivates me to continue to achieve and focus on living this lifestyle that I desire and deserve to live. What you prioritize is what your life will reflect, so make sure you are prioritizing the things that bring you joy and happiness.

Everything that I have achieved started with changing my perspective and focusing on what was possible instead of labeling it as impossible. Now let's focus on how shifting your perspective can help improve your relationships with others.

CREATING AMAZING RELATIONSHIPS IN YOUR LIFE

Relationships with individuals throughout your life are going to be complicated. You may find that someone challenges you, while another person provides unconditional support. As you are making amazing changes and shifts in your life, you need to shape your personal inner circle to find those who will challenge you and support you, even as you do the same for them.

Think about the people who surround you now. Do they support you on your journey of growth? Do they hold you accountable when you start to slip back into the status quo or that old way of thinking and behaving? If you want to create a major shift in your life, then you need those individuals to hold you accountable and to be honest with you.

Staying true to ourselves morally and ethically is not always easy when we surround ourselves with those who do not subscribe to our morals and ethics. Those within your inner circle are going to have the most profound impact on your thinking and actions.

As part of your journey to building your inner circle, it is important to clarify what you want to achieve in your life. Remember to focus on yourself. The best relationship, the best friendship you have, is the relationship you have with yourself. Self-mastery is key in figuring out how to live a purposeful life.

I embraced my dreams by initially writing them down. For example, I purchased my first home on my own, took a trip to Machu Picchu and the Galapagos Islands, and revolved my schedule around volunteering at events I always wanted to partake in. I achieved these dreams, but the timeframe was a lot longer than predicted.

Where do you want to go? What do you want to see and experience? The world is large and there are plenty of places to see, cultures to explore and experience, and food to try. Another benefit of traveling is that you build confidence in your abilities, be it to navigate travelling in a foreign country or conquering a mountain. Start crossing things off your bucket list or else you'll find yourself with a long list that was never accomplished.

Be open to new experiences and allow yourself to enjoy a variety of what life has to offer. It's the best way to truly discover yourself. It's time to stop existing and start living a fun and enjoyable life. When you purposefully plan the type of life you want and share with the world how you want to be treated, then people will respond.

Take a piece of paper and spend a few minutes thinking about everything that you want to accomplish in your life. Don't put timeframes on it. Goals and milestones move you forward in your life and can help you achieve what is necessary to transition through different life stages. A bucket list is based around experiences and moments that you want to have as part of your life's journey.

CREATE FINANCIAL INDEPENDENCE

Another part of perspective thinking is homeownership. Some individuals have different ideas regarding owning property, but the truth is that homeownership is key to building your net worth.

Financially, I had to be frugal to accomplish my goals of becoming an entrepreneur and homeowner. When you have a greater purpose, a greater "why" for your shift in perspective, and a greater reason why you are doing what you are doing, then everything else becomes irrelevant.

Being worried about money and driven to make more can lead to an obsession at the level that you will ignore your loved ones, your health, and your well-being. I did exactly that, constantly burnt out to prove that I could make it in the corporate world. Keeping up an image that I didn't want to be known for.

You can move yourself forward financially if you take responsibility for your choices and take control of how you are using your assets. If it seems as if you are sabotaging yourself financially, then you might want to stop and explore your attitude regarding money. Often, your struggles to stay on budget, control your spending, or save to invest can be wrapped up in beliefs about money that have burrowed into your subconscious and become part of the spending choices you make on a daily basis.

The way money and financial matters were presented when you were younger impacts your financial perspective today. The last financial recession had a major impact on many families and their finances. For the people this affected, their goal now may be to take fewer financial risks to avoid having that experience happen to them again.

If you look back to those who grew up during the Great Depression, they often struggled to spend money on anything, even when they clearly needed it. These individuals had lived through traumatic financial experiences, so their future choices of not wanting to put money in banks or to live very frugally were understandable. If your grandparents were raised in that era, they may have passed some of those beliefs or fears onto you.

What are your beliefs about money? How you view money and the beliefs behind those views will help you to appreciate why you make certain financial decisions. If you don't figure out the underlying cause, you will be unable to fix it. Instead, you will simply manage the symptoms, which is not the best long-term solution.

THE POWER IN WRITING

Throughout this chapter, you have learned the value in shifting your perspective. There are many fantastic opportunities in life if you explore with curiosity.

It is possible to heal from the past and move confidently into your future. Find ways to move, act, and create motion within your life. Working with a life coach can support you in your self-discovery journey. I help both men and women who are fitness enthusiasts and business owners to achieve their goals by focusing on successful habits, mindsets, wellbeing, nutrition, fitness, and relationships. I want to tell you that it is possible to heal from the past and live a better life starting today. You deserve to live your dream lifestyle now. Contact Andrea Ngui at www.herovi.coach.

Start by creating steppingstones to put yourself in a position to leap into the life you always wanted to live. Intention and deliberate actions are key to shifting your perspective.

Let's put perspective thinking into perspective. For example, whether it's a testimonial on LinkedIn, feedback on a report, a critique of a movie, a biography for a speaking engagement, or an opinion of a product on Amazon, they usually all have a more thoroughly written response than a verbal response. You know what I am saying?

Articulating your message by writing it down, or typing it out, has a profound effect on your level of perspective thinking. It helps heighten your level of awareness, level of learning, level of maturity, and level of wisdom. So, will you be writing things down on paper or on an electronic device?

Social media platforms are great tools in training your brain to ensure you are as articulate as possible with your message. Your message should be clear and concise with the knowledge you want others to read. You want to minimize the range of misinterpretation.

When it comes to complex things in life, how can you figure things out if you can't even articulate yourself proficiently by initially writing them down?

Don't get hung up on the agonizingly annoying feeling that the process will take too long. The length of time is irrelevant. Doing a half fast job leaves you stuck in a repetitive loophole with the illusion of the falsehood that you solved the issue. Writing it down and writing it out allows you to organize your thoughts. How can you expect to communicate clearly if you don't truly and entirely know what you want to say?

Expressing yourself by articulating your feelings with better words will help you get from where you are now to where you want to be. Eventually, it will help you create what you desire to achieve in life.

Creativity can be taught through perspective thinking. The television show Stranger Things has an upside-down world, which is another dimension of the universe. Songs, movies, quotes, clichés, and poetry all tend to have a deeper meaning than what the eye beholds on the surface. Has it ever happened to you when, over time, hearing the same clichés makes a new insight pop into your head? You start to wonder, "How did I miss that this entire time? I didn't know. I had no idea. Why didn't you tell me before?" Seeing things from another angle, from the inside out, and elevating your level of thinking helps you improve in becoming a problem solver within your own life.

Preparation is key in achieving the result of success. As Eric Thomas, aka ET, says, "Fall in love with the process, and the results will come." Practice makes perfect. Do the training, drills, exercises, practices, and show up where you really need to grind it out.

Is this why athletes practice so much? To fine tune their athleticism? Could this be a success method in how people accomplish so much in a day? A successful habit to develop is to intentionally think about embracing a continuous higher level of awareness with everything. It all starts with your level of perspective thinking. Life will start to unfold with what you deserve, and you will reap what you sow. Let this glimpse into how I shifted my perspective inspire you to do the same.

Contact Andrea Ngui at **www.herovi.coach** to learn how you can work together as you shift your perspective thinking and grow your business and personal lifestyle.

What Does Change Mean to You?

Fundamental Elements for a Vibrant, Fulfilling Life

TONY DEBOGORSKI

How do you view change? For many individuals, change has become something to fear. It invokes feelings of anxiety and potential loss. There is often little focus on what we can gain from change. Instead, the negative feelings and thought patterns overwhelm us, which can make change more difficult to accept and benefit from.

Think of the flight or fight response. Change, if we don't manage it effectively, can trigger that response. It can make us respond as if our lives are being threatened, when it's more likely that we are simply being affected by changing circumstances. Some of these circumstances are in our control and others are out of our control. However, if we can alter our reaction to change, then we can reap some amazing benefits.

Yes, you can benefit from change. However, in order to do so you need to be willing to create a new mindset in regards to how you view change and how you choose to act. Without the right mindset, you might be missing out on a change that could give depth to your life and the lives of those around you.

Changes, both those that happen to us and the ones that we create ourselves, have the potential to create new opportunities and experiences we might otherwise miss. These can give us another perspective and enrich our lives. Change did just that for me as a young man.

I grew up in rural Canada, where hard work and sweat were the building blocks of your success. I learned to be a jack of all trades, because that was the way you got things done around a farm. When I left to attend university, the idea was that I would end up coming home, marrying my high school girlfriend, and raising my family in the farming community where I was raised.

This step towards a university education was already a big change, since only a few of my family members actually went on to get a university education. Working hard was our way of life, and it was hard physical work. I couldn't imagine any other way, but university gave me a new way to live and introduced me to the idea of working smarter, not harder.

My life was enriched by not only the classes I attended, but the people I met. I was exposed to those who hadn't lived their entire life on a farm. I was exposed to different perspectives on how to tackle a variety of challenges. It altered my perception of the world, giving me a broader viewpoint. At the same time, I also deepened my appreciation of the values my parents instilled in me.

It was my first experience with change, but definitely not my last. I took the step to open my mind to change, which allowed me to get comfortable with the idea. During this time, I learned that it was okay to find assistance in accepting a change and acting on it without fear. The life I live today is defined by change. Now, instead of fear and anxiety, I welcome change for the blessings it may bring. How did I get to this point? It started with my willingness to learn and grew from there.

There is a process to change, but if we are not careful, we can actually prolong the process and make it more difficult. Let's walk through the reality of change. First, you have the old status quo. This is the reality of how things are right now. It could be a fairly peaceful way of life or you could find it difficult, but it is what you know.

Now a foreign element is introduced. It could be a new job or a move, for example. Most of the time, our first reaction is to resist, fearing the chaos that we are sure is to follow. After a point, we see the transforming idea of change and begin to integrate it into our lives. As time goes on, we then integrate the change into our lives and thus create a new status quo. Still, the impact of many aspects of this process can be lessened if we take a different point of view toward change.

Through mentors and my own experiences, I learned the key elements that can impact your ability to not only weather change, but thrive in the process. These five key elements are necessary to create the right mindset, one that embraces change, instead of being governed by a fear of change.

KEY #1. SELF-BELIEF

The first key is your belief in yourself. This is the foundation of a vibrant and fulfilling life. Without confidence in your own ability to handle challenges, you will see change as a crisis, instead of a benefit or an opportunity to grow as an individual.

Throughout our lives, we are told how to act, dress, and even think. Our belief systems are influenced by this training. In addition, as we grow older and other influences come into play from the world around us. Just take a moment and think about all the people and ideas you encounter on a daily basis. These could be teachers, family members, workmates, television, the internet, etc. The list goes on and on.

All of these influences are not focused on teaching us to think for ourselves, but instead are focused on developing our thinking to fall in line with who they believe we should be. Call it the social conditioning of our world. There often isn't time to learn who we are, to spend time with ourselves, to think, imagine, and explore the world. Instead, if we don't buy out the time, we can find that we are dissatisfied with our lives and unable to determine why.

We often have our purpose in life defined for us by others. This can lead to a lack of fulfillment in our lives, especially if what we are supposed to be doesn't fit our true vision of who we are.

The key is to stop and examine your belief system. Focus on your values. How many of them would you say you genuinely believe and how many have you taken on because of someone else in your life? It is amazing how many of our beliefs may no longer be serving us, but we are still using them to define ourselves and the world around us. Like the traditional fall and spring cleaning of our homes, we need to constantly be willing to clean the beliefs that no longer serve us or contribute to the growth and happiness of our lives from our consciousness.

Do you wake up in the morning satisfied with where you are in life? Can you look in the mirror and see a face excited to meet the day? Do you feel accountable for your life or does it feel as if your life is happening to you? How you see the world is based on your self-belief. What crafts your self-belief?

It hinges on your ability to see yourself master a skill and then be able to do it again and again successfully. Positive experiences help us grow our confidence in ourselves and define who we are. These moments often start in our early childhood, setting up a pattern throughout our lives.

My first memory of confidence building occurred when I was 11 years old. The regional elementary track and field meet was coming up. I wanted to win the top male athlete award. Although I had participated in the meet in the past, I hadn't won before. This time, I decided to do things differently. In preparation for the meet, I spent extra time training, including running after school. I was determined and my goal dominated my thoughts. It was a type of visualization, one that helped build my confidence going into the meet.

I had entered into five events and there were points for coming into first, second, and third place. On the day of the meet, it was sunny, the field and track were dry. Conditions were perfect for this outdoor event. My focus was on doing my best to earn the most points possible. At the end of the event, I had four first place ribbons and one for second place.

I was presented with the trophy for top male athlete. That feeling of accomplishment boosted my sense of what I could do and built my self-belief.

What goals have you set that you were able to accomplish on your own? How did you feel after you achieved your goal? Setting and accomplishing goals is a great way to feel better about yourself. How does this translate into having a different mindset about change? When you feel confidence in your abilities, you will not find yourself fearing change and the challenges it can present.

However, in the midst of a major change, you might find yourself neglecting your needs. How often do we put ourselves last when others around us are in need of our time and attention? While we might think that it will last for only a short period of time, putting ourselves on the back burner can become a routine, one that has a negative impact on our lives.

This can leave you worn out mentally and put you into a negative frame of mind. I can point to research and personal experiences to give you examples of why a negative mindset can be the anti-change and can encourage you to avoid thinking about the potential benefits of change. Once you focus on caring for your needs, you are in a better position to weather change and give assistance to others. Once you find confidence and strength in yourself and your abilities, you will be able to master whatever change and challenges come your way.

One important point is that you might still be afraid, but don't let it paralyze you into not acting at all. Remember those moments of success and allow them to motivate you to keep going. The keys to being self-reliant are perseverance, dedication, and integrity. When you have them, you will be able to conquer just about anything.

KEY #2. PURPOSE

Your life is a journey and you are the navigator. Some individuals choose to navigate based on their surroundings, essentially letting the waves aimlessly lead them along. In the end, that kind of life rarely leads to happiness with change or with yourself. You become a product of your circumstances, instead of defining yourself on your own terms.

What is purpose? According to the American Heritage Dictionary, it is "The object toward which one strives or for which something exists, an aim or a goal. The reason for which anything is done, created or exists, an aim or a goal."

When you examine your own life, are you excited about what you do? Could you define the purpose of your life? For some, their purpose becomes apparent when they are young. They find the passion that defines their lives and shapes their careers. Others never find that purpose, leaving them to struggle to find satisfaction with their lives.

If you haven't defined the purpose of your life, then it is time to think about what you enjoy. What sparks your passion? What gets you excited to get out of bed in the morning? Once you start to define your purpose, set your goals around what you enjoy. This can help you gain perspective on your purpose.

However, keep in mind that your purpose is not set in stone. It can change over time as you gain life experience and a better understanding of yourself. Taking action will help you be drawn to what you like. Try new things. Consider the spiritual influences in your life. To postulate is the act of creation. It can happen when you think, write, or speak something into being. Focus, because if you think it, then you can do it.

Change can be initiated by you. It doesn't have to be dominated by circumstances outside of your control. You can start by taking one action that will move you closer to a specific goal. That goal could be to simply change your way of thinking or to release a belief that is no longer serving you, but could be limiting you instead.

With your purpose defined, you could move forward to produce the life you want and mindset for change, which starts with how you take care of yourself.

KEY #3. HEALTH

Fear and anxiety can have physical repercussions. They impact how our bodies feel, as well as our ability to fight off illnesses and deal with chronic conditions. Research has proven time and again that our minds can influence our physical well-being.

Are you poisoning your body through the negative thoughts you are dwelling on? To create the energy necessary for a vibrant fulfilling life you need to maximize your mental state, maintain your physical body, and nourish yourself properly. Keep your mind focused on what is possible, instead of focusing on what can't be done or any potentially negative consequences.

The combination of your mind and body is a synergistic relationship. It means you need to take care of both to achieve overall well-being. To start, let's focus on your physical body. Are you getting out on a regular basis to exercise and stretch your muscles? Do you raise your heart rate? One of the interesting side effects of physical activity is how it can impact our mood. When we are uplifted in mood, it translates into our thought processes. Regular physical exercise can contribute to greater overall positivity in our lives.

If you find it hard to get out on your own and get physically active, then consider finding a support group, a partner, or even a gym where you can be held accountable for showing up and putting in the effort. You will appreciate the results in terms of your health, making it worth the effort. Additionally, the physical benefits will allow you to grow in other areas of your life, thus making change more welcome, especially as your body grows stronger.

When it comes to your physical well-being, the reality is that you are what you put into your body. If you don't fuel your body for optimal performance, then it can't give you the very best physically. That can have a domino effect on how you operate mentally. When you are tired and not feeling your best, can you honestly say that you have made your best decisions? Or do you find yourself rethinking those choices at a later date?

There are five products, which I refer to as the five white poisons, that you need to be aware of. They can be found in a variety of foods throughout your local grocery store. So much of what we eat today has been processed extensively, removing the natural nutrients and fiber-rich parts. As a result, we are exposed to more of these five products than ever before. What are these five white poisons? Sugar, starch, flour, salt, and milk.

All of these are foods that need to be consumed in moderation. Recognize that they are often hidden ingredients within other foods. Therefore, it is wise to limit your intake wherever possible to make sure you aren't putting too much of these items into your body.

Part of your physical health is also caring for your brain. Think of it as a muscle. Like every muscle in your body, it is important to allow it to relax and get the necessary rest. This can be done through meditation or even finding some quiet time away from your family and friends to relax and think quietly without distraction. Doing so also allows you to reduce your stress level. Making sure your stress level comes down will positively impact your mental health as well.

Do you have a place that brings you peace? Having this place allows you to mentally unwind and just let go of your stress, even if it is just temporarily. Meditation is a method that you can use, even if all you can do is go to a quiet place in your home or office. There are a variety of meditation techniques available. Some individuals prefer a calming form of music to accompany their meditation, while others prefer to just enjoy the silence. Whatever you prefer, the point is to make your mental health a priority. If you do, it will be much easier to handle change and thrive.

Change can bring benefits and give us opportunities we might not otherwise have considered without the upheaval in our lives. But in order to benefit from change, we need to maintain our positivity, both physically and mentally. This can be hard to do when a change has a particularly emotional impact. Relying on family and friends for support is key to dealing with the more emotional aspects of any change in your life.

Throughout this discussion of your health, I haven't really touched on one area that impacts our well-being. That is our relationships. But how do they impact our lives and what do we need to remember about these relationships when it comes to change?

KEY #4. RELATIONSHIPS

Did you know that you are shaped by the people you spend the most time with? Those individuals will influence your ideas, beliefs, and actions. This also extends to your attitude. If you are surrounded by positive thinkers, it is much easier to maintain a positive attitude. Think about the last time you were surrounded by negative individuals. After a while, did it seem as if that negative and critical spirit rubbed off on you?

Here are some questions to ask yourself about the people you spend time with. Are they primarily positive or negative? Do you find yourself having spirited conversations with plenty of give and take, or do you find that you are just a dumping ground for all their complaints about life?

If you want to create change in your life or be more accepting of the changes in your life, then you may need to assess who you spend most of your time with. Creating a new attitude or shifting your thought process means assessing who is influencing them both and whether that influence is helping or hurting.

When I was finishing my university education, I was associating with a group of friends who were eager to join the corporate world. I had worked in the corporate world during my summer breaks, but I had also started a business installing sprinkler systems in areas where there was new home construction. I did this after hours and on weekends. Although I was working a lot, I was also figuring out that I didn't have to go the corporate route to be successful. My small part-time business had made me more money than my daily corporate job.

Our final year of school came and, of course, my friends and I discussed what our next steps were as we started life after university. Some had mixed feelings about what direction to take after graduating. The options included attempting to open a business in the role of entrepreneur or applying to one of the many companies out there for a traditional corporate role.

Since most of my friends decided to go the corporate route, I did too, even though my experience indicated that I could be equally, if not more, successful in the role of entrepreneur. The individuals I associated with provided acknowledgement and support during that decision-making period of my life.

Are there some decisions where you can see the influence of your associates? Can you look back now and see that perhaps a different decision would have been more appropriate for the path you ultimately wanted to pursue?

While we all want to think that we are independent thinkers, sudden influences from our associates can impact what we choose to do and how we think and act. Yet, with a greater understanding of who you are as a person (your goals and your passions), you will find that you can truly be an independent thinker and identify the effect of those influences around you.

Self-knowledge takes time, but the reward is a better way to embrace life and the change around us, both personally and professionally. If you want to move down a specific path toward your goal, you need to make sure to associate with like-minded individuals. They can encourage and support you as you work to achieve those specific milestones.

As you discover what you are passionate about, you will be able to find like-minded friends and associates who are focused on that particular activity or pursuit. For instance, you may be passionate about helping young people. There may be local groups geared toward providing activities and mentorship to teenagers within your community. Getting involved in those groups will put you around others who share your passion, which can help motivate you even further.

Take the time to examine your beliefs and determine if the friends you are associating with are the right people to support you in the next stage or season of your life. Not everyone you spend time with will be an active part of helping you achieve your goals. However, they can be the individuals who make you laugh, as well as help you see the positive when situations or circumstances seem overwhelming.

The point is to be around people who embrace change and can help you to do the same. When it comes to your mindset, negative association will eventually bring even the most positive mindset down. Have you ever tried to accomplish something that you had already decided was impossible? It becomes an uphill battle, and you likely didn't succeed.

A positive attitude, on the other hand, makes it possible for you to achieve even more than you thought was possible. In addition, your positive mindset could have an influence on those around you. Imagine being a positive influence to those who are important to you. The best relationships are the ones where you both are actively working to support and encourage each other in pursuit of your passions, while being there for each other during times of major change or upheaval that life seems to throw at us all.

If you are looking to make adjustments to your circle of friends and associates, consider looking into your community for opportunities to meet new people. Some ideas include joining a club or charity organization. If there is an activity that you have been interested in trying, why not sign up for lessons? What things have you been afraid to try for one reason or another? Why not give one of those things a try? If your fear is that you won't do well, make peace with that and do it anyway. You might find that as you conquer your fear, you make new friends that will enrich your life.

I want to point out here that the idea is to make you better able to adapt to change and train yourself to see the benefit of change versus focusing on the fear and anxiety. Each of these new experiences is putting you in charge of creating change in your life on a smaller scale, which will make it easier for you to handle change on a larger scale.

The most rewarding sport even for me was signing up and participating in triathlons. I was a prairie boy who didn't grow up around water. Signing up for a triathlon forced me to learn how to swim. I could have let fear of the unknown stop me, but instead I broadened my horizons.

Additionally, I signed up with a friend. We challenged each other and held each other accountable for attaining our goals. It was not an easy journey, but I found new strength as I pushed myself and supported my friend.

The 10-month journey before my first triathlon was grueling at times. It included swim lessons, getting the proper equipment, the proper bike, the right shoes, and more. After those 10 months of training, lessons, and standing up to my own fears, the day of the race finally came.

The first leg of the triathlon was swimming, which I can definitely say was not my strength. In fact, when I ran into the water, I was with a pack of men, but after a few minutes of kicking and banging around, I was alone and about ready to give up. Instead of doing that, I pulled back for a moment, composed myself, and then started to swim, concentrating on one stroke at a time.

I finished dead last in the swim, but at least I finished. I continued with ease to do the bike and run, completing those two legs in top times. I was dead last overall, because of my slow swim, but I still felt a great sense of accomplishment because I had completed my goal. In the process, I had met many new people who shared an interest in triathlons. I also got closer to my friend Nick, who trained with me and completed the same triathlon.

It was a rewarding event for me, not only because I actually finished what I set out to do, but because when I went out to celebrate that night, I met my future wife. Our relationship has been full of change and challenges, but none of the joys would have been possible if I hadn't stepped outside of my comfort zone to try something new and conquered a fear at the same time.

Think about the various relationships in your life. Could there be someone who is already in your life who would be supportive as you step outside your comfort zone? Those individuals are the ones who will support you through change. They are key relationships to nurture. Still, those relationships will not be able to support you if you are not able to communicate your needs to those critical people in your life. As a result, my fifth key is also the most critical: communication.

KEY #5. COMMUNICATION

No matter who we are and what we do throughout the day, we are constantly communicating. We use our faces, our hands, and, of course, our speech to communicate what we are thinking and feeling on a daily basis.

Yet within the realm of communication, the opportunities for misunderstandings abound. There are literally hundreds of thousands of examples throughout history demonstrating how misunderstandings can grow into much larger breakdowns of relationships between individuals, groups, and even countries.

Communication is truly an incredible concept. Great communicators can wow us and bring difficult concepts or ideas into focus. Have you ever heard the speeches of Martin Luther King Jr.? Decades after his passing, his words continue to move people. Then there are more current examples, such as Tony Robbins, Bob Proctor, or Brian Tracy. All of these individuals are amazing in their delivery of self-help information. Listen to their presentations and you can see how they really connect with their audiences.

Change requires communication, but change doesn't go over well if it is not communicated well. Every parent who communicates with a teenager can appreciate this point. Their child may not be able to articulate their frustration or the reasons behind it. An argument often becomes par for the course, leaving everyone frustrated and out of sorts. Misunderstandings can make change difficult to handle, because you may not understand why the change is occurring.

Companies often make this mistake as well. They may not clearly communicate their vision, so when they make changes, their employees are often left feeling frustrated and out of the loop. It can also make them feel uncertain about their job security, which can negatively impact their productivity. The reality is that miscommunication can have a large impact on whether change is welcomed or feared.

Communication is more than just speaking clearly. It is listening to and understanding the concerns of the other person and doing your best to address those concerns. When it comes to creating change in your life, you may find that you need to explain to your family why you are making that change. How do you communicate your choice? Often, how well it is communicated is reflected in the level of support you receive and if the change is embraced or not.

Have you been part of a change where the communication was less than you expected? How did that impact your ability to accept the change and create something incredible from that opportunity? For many of us, the answer is that the change was more difficult and we likely didn't support it wholeheartedly.

Again, the point is that communication can make a change easier to accept or a lack of it can make the implementation of a change more difficult. If you are initiating change in your own life, be sure that you are clearly communicating your needs to those around you. While they may not always agree with your decisions, they are much more likely to support them and the changes you want to make if you can clearly communicate the change and its impact.

Along with good communication, you need to be a good listener. Often misunderstandings occur because one individual is not really listening to the other. They may miss key instructions or details that could make the situation clearer. As a result, it can be easy to act without truly knowing all the necessary facts and circumstances. Can you see how not listening well could impact how you feel about a change in your life? It is also easy to see how others might be less supportive of change you initiate if they weren't listening.

How can you tell if someone is truly hearing you? Ask them questions and then clarify when it appears that they may not have gotten an accurate picture of what is about to occur. Some individuals may want to willfully misunderstand, and you want to do everything in your power to avoid that. At the same time, be a good listener. Don't listen to respond, but listen to understand their concerns, worries, and potential fears. Make adjustments to address their concerns where possible, but be as reassuring as you can when those adjustments might not be possible.

When you don't listen, you run the risk of missing key instructions or information that could directly impact your life or the change you are about to make.

I was always working, even from a young age. For a period of time, I worked on a gravel crusher as a ground person. My job was to go around and check for broken wheels, conveyors, and signs of wear and tear on other components. If something was wrong, I was to report it immediately to the tower person overseeing the operation. His job was to shut down the entire mechanical operation so the problem could be addressed. If he didn't, a major failure could occur, which could end up costing thousands of dollars of damage.

One morning, I was tired and didn't pay attention when I was relieving the previous shift. I had missed that a flashing was tearing and did not report it. An hour later, that flashing tore through. My boss saw it first. Gravel was everywhere. He had the operation stopped, then came over to the tool shack to fire me for not properly checking the system. That miscommunication cost the company time and money, plus I lost my job. The lesson? Communication and paying attention to the details is key to success in any area of your life, but especially when you are initiating major change.

Now let's talk about how a lack of communication can contribute to conflict. Our ability to connect with others can be hampered if we don't communicate well or if we are not sensitive to their needs and hot spots. Our personal and professional lives can be impacted by poor communication.

If you are considering acting to make changes in your life, start with how you communicate with others. We can all find areas to improve and make our connections with others deeper and more meaningful. The art of language is not easy. From birth, we are trained to communicate, but it doesn't come easily to all of us. Some become better than others at expressing themselves. The art of communication can be terrifying and amazing at the same time. You may also find it difficult to express yourself, especially when dealing with loved ones. How can you communicate more effectively with the individuals in your life?

Start by asking questions. This helps you gather information. Repeat back to the speaker your understanding of what they just said in response to your question. If they don't agree with your interpretation, keep asking for clarification until you get it. Be sure that you genuinely listen to the response before you start making assumptions. Try and imagine the situation from the other person's point of view. Be patient, because the best communication takes time.

There are also classes on public speaking and the art of communication. If you find yourself struggling consistently in this area, consider taking a course. The principles and real-world practice can help you improve your general communication skills. If you find yourself losing your train of thought, then consider writing down what you want to say. Be clear and concise where possible. Then use your written thoughts as a platform to bring up various points when appropriate within the context of the conversation.

Don't underestimate the power of practicing your communication skills in front of a mirror. This is where you can work on eye contact, exploring your various facial expressions, and also how to speak clearly. If you can talk to yourself, then it will get easier to talk to others. Make an effort to come out of your comfort zone, especially if you are not a good communicator. Consider it a change for the better.

Recognize that by improving your communication skills you can improve the quality of your life, as well as weather changing circumstances more effectively.

MOVE FORWARD WITH ME

Throughout this chapter, I have focused on some key areas that can make change more palatable, and reduce the fear and anxiety that commonly occurs. Still, the reality is that change, especially change we didn't initiate, can be overwhelming. Over the course of my lifetime, I have dealt with a variety of changes and I can say that not every experience was pleasant. But they all taught me valuable lessons.

I also want to remind you that change doesn't need to be something that occurs to you, but can be something you initiate. Consider areas of your life that are not as satisfying as you would like them to be. For example, are you struggling financially, but find yourself reluctant to make changes or take the risks necessary to turn your financial life around? Here is an area where making a change happen can have a significant impact.

However, don't limit yourself merely to material affluence. There are literally dozens of areas where you could find yourself hesitating to make changes. No matter what change you want to make, the mindset you choose will determine whether the change is successful or a struggle.

Throughout my work with individuals on changes in their lives, one thing has become clear; your mindset is key to making change work for you and allowing yourself to embrace change effectively.

I'm willing to work with you to help create the change that you want to see in your life. Let's face it, changes to our self-belief can lead to even more significant changes in other areas of our lives. With an improvement to your self-belief, there is no telling what you can accomplish. The changes to your point of view about yourself and what you can accomplish will help you make different choices about how you choose to live and work.

I believe that coaching is key to creating the right mindset to initiate and absorb changes in your life. A positive mindset allows you to see change in terms of what is possible, instead of focusing on the potential losses. Until you take the leap, you will never know exactly what is possible. But it can be hard to take those first steps to overhauling your thought process on your own.

I believe strongly in coaching and mentorship. It is a way to pass on the wisdom you have learned and the key strategies you may have discovered for addressing and initiating change. As part of my efforts to help others embrace change, my coaching and mentorship is available to you.

In my book, The Book of Change, I tackle a variety of topics and areas where you can start making small changes to build up to bigger ones. I also discuss how you can take dramatic and difficult circumstances and use them to learn and grow.

Using these tools, you can make a difference in your own life and in the lives of others. You can go from being fearful of change to being an example of embracing change for those in your family, your social circle, and your community. However, coaching isn't the only way to work on your skills to create and embrace change.

You can become a change advocate. That means allowing your positive mindset regarding change to influence others and impact their attitudes toward possible changes in their own lives. Your own example of dealing with change can serve as inspiration for others, which can then allow them to turn themselves into change advocates. It is a never ending cycle, which can give you peace of mind, even when faced with the toughest of challenges.

Additionally, there are other key takeaways for you to keep in mind as you start the journey to create change in your life. One way to embrace it is to understand what is happening and even to learn why.

Continuing education allows you to take the fear out of any change. After all, most of the fear of change stems from a lack of knowledge about what the change will mean for you, your family, and your community. When we are informed, change can be less intimidating, which can make us less fearful and more willing to take risks. Change is a part of taking risks to grow and explore our passions, achieve our goals, and fulfill our dreams. Without the right information and mindset, we will be unwilling to take the risks needed to achieve everything we imagine possible.

Clearly, you need to remember that change is a constant in your life. No one can escape it, no matter how risk adverse they may be. You need to embrace change for the benefits it can provide by creating a different mindset, gaining new skills, or even just acknowledging the personal growth that has resulted.

The change you see in your lifetime can and likely will have a profound impact on the lives of others, both now and in the future. Respect the people around you and demonstrate love and support when they are faced with changes, both large and small.

Contact me at **tony@tonydebogorski.com**. I would love to explore the ways that I can help you create real change in your life through adjustments to your mindset and increasing your willingness to learn and explore. Be inspired to create the meaningful life that you have always wanted and step away from living in fear of the unknown.

Amazing things are waiting for you! It is time for you to take the first step towards being a change agent in your own life.

Break Down the Box

Taking a Risk to Create an Amazing Life

KIRK JAKESTA

Become who you were meant to be.

Listen to that voice in the back of your head that says, "I could do this."

Growing up as a young man, I quickly adapted to the lifestyle that was presented to me, a life that threatened to consume me, sending me into the dark path of life if I were to let it. Where the thought of change was not possible, not for me.

Perhaps you grew up in a lifestyle like mine where drug and alcohol abuse were the norm, where selling drugs as a young adolescent wasn't unusual but accepted, or you grew up in a good wholesome environment where life just made you comfortable with what you had. Deep down, we always want more. We want the best that life has to offer. In the back of our mind, our thoughts tell us that we are not worthy of it. We deal with the hand life dealt us and face the tough financial challenges without a leg to stand on, believing that we are not worthy of better.

Just getting by was my specialty, and still is. It was my normal growing up. My soon to be 75-year-old father is still working camp jobs as an excavator operator to this day, going in and out of retirement for the past 5 years, despite health limiting him from being able to see or hear properly. All this simply to make sure that he and my mother can have the basics. My mother is one of my best friends, next to my little love Aiyanna, who will turn 6 this year, and the love of my life, Amanda.

At 56, my mother suffers from rheumatoid arthritis and osteoporosis. Seeing your parents' heath deteriorate, especially after growing up thinking they were bullet proof, is a hard pill to swallow. My parents have been the best. They don't assume that they deserve much, so they don't reach for anything more, and honestly feel it's to late. That's where I want to step in. They gave me a good life. Despite growing up the way I did, my parents have been my crutch, and shaped me into the man I am today, along with the influence of my brothers and grandparents.

We all have close friends and family, whose aging has brought the reality of losing them closer to mind. Many of us have lost close family and friends to sudden loss. Tomorrow is never promised, and the best time to create a life worth living is NOW. My loved ones inspired me, and I want to inspire those who need it. To show that no matter where you are in life, there is always a fork in the road. If you are brave enough to look past the dark scary cover of it, then you will realize that life's greatest experiences are usually on the other side of fear. I want you to recognize that you deserve to tap into the greatness inside you! There is something more than the scraps of life. There is an amazing banquet, but if you don't respond to the invitation, then you will never be able to enjoy the feast.

The last year has brought some amazing opportunities my way, but first, I had to accept my invitation to the banquet. I had to take action and show up to reap the benefits. I'll admit, it took a major shift in my thinking, and it's a constant battle against procrastination, self-doubt and fear of failure. Even as I write this chapter, I realize that it took a lot to get to this point. I had to crawl out of that hole of self-pity, dust myself off and get back into the game. I needed to step beyond what I saw as possible in my everyday life, and instead believe that I had a greatness that could propel me forward if I was willing to take that leap of faith to create significant change.

Starting with my first self-development program and the potential for an amazing compensation plan, a seed was planted in me. I gained the mindset to be my own boss one day. To stop working 8-10 hours a day on another man's dream. When we think about how much free time we have, how much of it is wasted? Think about it; the average person sleeps 8 hours a day and works for 8 hours a day. That's 16 hours dedicated to sustaining a living and getting the proper sleep. There are 8 remaining hours that most of us aren't taking full advantage of. I know there are other essential activities that are accounted for in those 8 remaining hours, but you get the gist of it. I came to recognize that I could make my life extraordinary, but I NEEDED TO CHANGE MY MINDSET to tap into my ability. One of the hardest people you will ever have to battle is yourself.

Imagine stepping out on faith like that in your life. Having a vision for your future and then taking a leap without the proverbial safety net. My leap led me to many mentors; a self-development course through my now professional family, the Matrix group; an opportunity to begin exploring real estate investing by taking a few reputable courses; and of course, taking the leap and jumping into a book deal with an amazing powerhouse, world renowned speakers, authors, entrepreneurs, and now my co-authors, with the goal to pursue a speaking career to inspire First Nations people around the world. Note that all those opportunities gave back to me in a big way. They helped me to mentally prepare for the next opportunity, the next open door, and the next chapter in my journey towards an amazing life.

Each step I took led me to another networking opportunity, another inspiration, another mentor, and the momentum continues to build. I put myself on the path to find those "once in a lifetime" opportunities. Now I want to reach out to my people, becoming a role model and demonstrating that all things are possible. There is a life outside of your conditions, which is the reverse of the way you are living. It is possible to create a brighter future, but it starts with believing in yourself. Dedicate yourself to something, then great things will happen. You do not have to be a victim of your circumstances. Instead, you can take charge and be the change in your life.

You do not have to remain trapped by your ancestors' unfortunate past of residential school, and the horrible ripple effect of what they went through. For those who don't understand what they went through, that ripple effect has affected their children down through the generations in one way or the other. Now is the time to stop that ripple effect by making conscious choices in our lives to create change.

We must take responsibility for our past choices and actions, but more importantly, the ones we are making in the present. The present is all you can change, but the possibilities are endless if you are willing to move through the fear of the unknown and the fear of failure.

The point I want to make throughout this chapter is that you have the power to create, to build, and to change. It all starts with a willingness to open your mind to the possibilities and even to take risks to achieve what you have always dreamed of, even if you may have denied your ability to create that vision in the past.

I am here to tell you that all things are possible. You do not have to struggle through an endless loop of paychecks, overwhelming debt, and the hardship of not having the necessities. You do not have to let a troubled past get in the way of your amazing future. Instead, you can have a life that is rich in personal meaning and leaves a legacy behind for your children and grandchildren.

CULTURE IS THE FOUNDATION FOR GROWTH

Our culture is one based on close-knit families and time-honored traditions. For hundreds of years, we lived in harmony with the land and each other. Time has changed things, and modern life does not seem to focus on this rich cultural heritage. I even find that the way I was raised limited my access to my culture, disconnecting me from what should be a greater part of my life, although I believe strongly that it is never too late to learn and make it a part of my family's life. I will continue to put forth the effort to make that happen even if it's with only little snippets throughout our lives.

What cultural heritage am I referring to? I am First Nations. I represent Nisga'a Nation, from the village of Gitlaxt'aamiks or New Aiyansh, and from my father's side. I am part of the Tahltan Nation. These are parts of who I am, although I truly wish the connection with these cultures was an even stronger part of my daily life. Still, it doesn't stop me from being who I am.

Why isn't it a greater part of my life? My childhood was not easy. I would say that I was undereducated, as the school system in my village was rated the second lowest in British Columbia. On top of that, we had a house built in the early 2000's. A few years after we moved in, we had a kitchen fire. It did a lot of smoke damage to the kitchen, leaving it completely charred. Nothing was done to fix it. That is a mindset that I grew up with, one where you learned to live with what you had. There wasn't an expectation that we deserved to have the kitchen fixed and, 15 years after the fire, that damage is still there. This is the reality of where I came from and who I am. So, you can see why I would want more out of life.

What about your own life? Can you see places where damage was done, but you did nothing to fix it? All of us deal with some type of psychological, physical, or emotional trauma. It could be a result of choices we made, or the actions of others that were not in our control. This world is a cruel place. In the end, however, it is up to you to decide if you want to live as a victim or be a victor instead.

Growing up with my two older brothers, I was confronted with circumstances that I could have blamed for my life choices. At home, there was a lot of fighting, drinking, and smoking weed. It was a tough environment for a young adolescent but that was my normal. Around 15 or 16 years old, I went from being a recreational marijuana smoker to dealing the herb. In fact, I became one of the biggest weed dealers in the community at one point. Then I moved to hustling harder drugs, to the point where I was making good money for a teenager. I didn't feel that great about myself or what I was doing to get that money. However, the lifestyle was so different from the years that my family struggled that it was hard to turn my back on the money.

That all changed the day that one of my friends offered herself to me as payment for drugs. It felt like an incredibly low point in my life. I started asking myself what I was doing. This was not who I was meant to be. I was completely shocked by her offer, and I couldn't accept it. I ended up giving her the drugs for nothing and quitting that business. I was done contributing to tearing down myself and others. Now I had to figure out how I was going to build myself back up and, in the process, how I could help others do the same. The answers were still a few years away, but I was at least on the track to finding them.

If I had not stopped then, I could have ended up in jail, dead, or with the death of someone else on my conscience. Your choices create your future. By making the choice to get out of that life, I changed my own future and I am grateful for it. I learned at a young age that life is truly about moments. Moments where you can either take the path less taken or the familiar one. Even though I didn't acknowledge it back then, I was making these life-changing decisions. I can see now that my conscience was in the right place.

That rough environment offered few opportunities for young people like me. As I got out of the drug world, I realized that I couldn't stay where I was. I needed to create an opportunity for myself. So, I headed to Vancouver, where I attended Vancouver Island University Trade School. I took classes to be an automotive service technician. After graduating, it became clear that this wasn't the future for me either. The men in the trade hated their jobs, and I realized I didn't want to be one of them. I was at peace with that. Even though I dedicated almost a year of my life to achieve that certification, I knew deep down I couldn't sacrifice my life to unfulfillment and regret.

I felt as if I was going through the process of elimination. The knowledge about what didn't work for me was as valuable as the knowledge about what did work for me. I started to understand myself better and believe that my happiness was mine to create.

CREATING HAPPINESS STARTS WITH YOU

Happiness is not going to magically appear because of the things you own or the fact that you work 60 to 80 hours a week to bring home a paycheck. Instead, happiness is a state of mind, one that you can create, no matter your circumstances.

My determination to create change in my life led me to leave behind a life of drug dealing, and countless dead-end jobs. For the past 8 years, I have lived in Vancouver, where I started to do all kinds of different work, exploring my interests and trying to find my place in this world. I learned a lot about what I was good at, what I was okay at, and what I just struggled to accomplish.

During this time of exploration, I was still a typical young man, out to meet girls. They might not have been the girls that I could take home, but it was the life of a young man with few responsibilities. Then my daughter was born. She is my biggest inspiration, and I knew that I wanted to give her a better life than the one I had. Now I was inspired to do better, even if I wasn't sure how. I believed that if I did almost everything in the opposite way I was raised, I was going to be fine. In order to do that, I needed a new set of skills, and I needed a new way of thinking about the world and my place in it.

It was about becoming the role model that I wish I had when I was growing up, and finding inspiration in the young girl that now depended on me. To give her happiness, I had to be willing to claim it for myself to be able to provide a better life for her and my entire family. I'm a strong believer in "When I make it, we all make it."

Your happiness is a state of mind. You are in charge of your mind, not your circumstances. You can choose what to dwell on, and your point of view. I want to challenge you to recognize that you need to change your mindset about the circumstances themselves, thus creating happiness for yourself no matter where life currently has planted you.

IS NEGATIVE THINKING HOLDING YOU BACK?

Some individuals seem to naturally be able to find the silver lining of any situation, and their joy in life is apparent. Even when they are faced with difficult circumstances, they focus on what they can learn and how they can grow, instead of becoming defeated. Granted, that does not come naturally to everyone. In fact, many of us are quick to fall into a negative way of thinking, one that keeps us focused on what has gone wrong and keeps us from acting decisively.

The reason I point this out is because if you want to achieve real change in your life, you need to be able to act decisively. A negative mindset will keep you from acting, simply because you will spend all your time talking yourself out of doing anything. The excuses can be numerous. Here are just a few:

- I don't have the money.

- I don't have the education.

- I don't have the skills.

- Those adventures are for other people. I have a family to take care of.

- The risk is just too great.

Negative thinking means that you tend to value the risk higher than the

97

reward, so you freeze yourself in place, living with circumstances that you aren't excited about, simply because you can't accept the potential of risk.

Now if you aren't able to accept risk and you have a negative frame of mind, it can be very difficult to create the happiness you seek in your own life. It must start with a change to your own mindset, one that acknowledges risks but is not defined or held down by them. At the same time, I am not talking about a pie-in-the-sky type of thinking, the kind that cannot recognize challenges or potential issues.

Risk assessment is still a part of life, but the focus needs to be on how to mitigate the risk, not how to avoid acting so that you can avoid the risk altogether. When your mindset is in a positive frame, you are going to find that you look at risk differently. It is not an impasse or an obstacle that stops you from moving forward. Instead, you view it as something to be addressed, a challenge that can be navigated effectively. For every problem in life, there is a solution. The only thing that stops us is fear itself.

When you are focused on just surviving, and not on thriving, then no matter what soil you are planted in or the circumstances that you find yourself in, you are never going to be truly happy. In the quest for small moments of happiness, you are likely to make choices that are going to negatively impact yourself and those that you love.

Those choices could be anything, from drugs, alcohol, or even commitment issues. The point is that, long term, those choices are going to negatively impact your ability to make your situation better. Instead, you have now made your road even harder. Now you have another set of challenges to deal with, and those additional difficulties can be truly crushing to your mind and spirit.

Can you relate to some of these choices or ways of thinking? Can you understand negative thinking and using words like "can't," "won't," or "shouldn't" are keeping you from achieving what you were put on this earth to accomplish? As you can see, negative thinking can break down your spirit and leave you feeling as if you don't have the strength or ability to create change in your life. It can leave you feeling that your life is what it is, and you are better off just to accept it. I'm here to say f#!k that. Go Get Yours!

You are never truly stuck unless you choose to be. Can you find some light in the darkness, that inspiration and motivation you need to take the first step? I found it in my daughter, but it was also clear that I was changing my thinking and that was impacting my future in ways that I couldn't yet imagine.

MANIFESTING YOUR NEW REALITY STARTS WITH YOU

During the time before my daughter was born, I had that moment all new fathers do, questioning the finances and trying to figure out how to pay for this new miracle in my life.

My answer was civil construction, which led me to eventually becoming a heavy equipment operator. I picked up the experience needed by jumping into a piece of equipment every chance I got. Straight up, I manifested that into reality. I had it in my mind when I first stepped foot in the field as a laborer, watching the guys run those big machines, that one day "that would be me."

Are there areas in your life where you need to be aggressive to achieve a goal? I could have sat back and waited for someone to give me an opportunity to learn how to operate those machines, but the truth is, that day might never have come. By seizing the reins, I created the opportunities for myself and achieved my goal. It wasn't easy, and I had to make some sacrifices. For two years, I worked the night shift. Starting out as the lowest paid laborer (which was still good money for a new soon-to-be father) and working myself up to be a lead hand. Delegating tasks and executing them in a safe timely matter. Here is where my life revolved around eating, sleeping, and going to work. I couldn't do anything else, and it wasn't the healthiest lifestyle. But it was also the first time that I manifested one of my goals, and it wasn't going to be my last.

In spite of all that negative thinking from my past, I decided to take a leap beyond what I had already accomplished. I decided that I didn't have to work to barely make ends meet for the rest of my life. I did have the ability to leave something for my daughter, and I had the power to create a legacy, one that would impact the generations to follow. The question was how?

START WITH INSPIRATION AND ADD ACTION

No matter who you are and where you are in your life, there are individuals who inspire you. They are the ones who accomplish so much, despite the challenges and those who tell them that it can't be done. Yes, there are plenty of people out there who are going to tell you that nothing can change, you are risking too much, and that you will be sorry later. They might even claim that they are telling you these things for your own good, so that they can protect you.

That is not the kind of protection that you need. Instead, you need to be willing to take the risk, even be willing to fail. Fail forward. After all, if you never fail, then you will never know what it takes to succeed. You need to step beyond the opinions of others, beyond the fear, to have more, be more, and experience more.

To put it simply, failure is just a way of eliminating a process that wasn't going to work, thus allowing you to focus your time and energy on other options that might be more successful. At this point it is not a secret anymore. It's out in the open and has been for decades; failure is the crucial ingredient for success. You must treat each failure as part of the elimination process, one more step closer to achieving your goal. Eventually, something will give, and you will get the right idea or find the solution to your problem. This is a guaranteed result of dedicating your thoughts to your goal, and you best believe it works to the opposite effect as well. Your thoughts navigate your life. Whichever road you choose to go down is directly controlled by your own thoughts.

My goal was to achieve a better life for my family, and that meant figuring out what I was good at and what I wasn't good at. Simply choosing to abandon a course of action that isn't working can feel so liberating. Plus, every time you remove yourself from a course of action that isn't working, you are moving yourself closer to achieving your goals!

The inspiration for my next course change came as I realized that my mind was not fully in my work. I operate heavy machinery, which is not a job where you can afford to be distracted.

Instead, you need to stay focused on what you are doing and keeping the people around you safe as you complete the task at hand. Once I realized that I was in the place where I couldn't keep that level of focus, I knew I needed to take a break. It was my moment to take a leap and see where it would lead. I was inspired by several individuals, ones who took risks and were willing to give everything to make big changes in their lives.

Even though I am still working to this day after a bit of a hiatus, the skills that I picked up after all these years have given me the credibility to become a foreman after only two months coming back to the same line of work. That is a testament to the dedication that I once had to this specific line of work. Even though I know this won't be for the rest of my life, it feels good to know that I have what it takes to walk on to a new job, take control, and quickly establish myself in a key role.

What are you willing to give up? I bet you might be thinking that you aren't willing to give up much. Your life is comfortable, you have a routine, and even if it isn't everything that you hoped it would be, at least you understand the rules and expectations. That is where we all get tripped up from time to time. We choose the devil we know versus the devil we don't, because the unknown is scary. It is a dark hole and we don't know what might be hiding in there or lurking just around the corner. The truth is that what is lurking around the corner could be amazing, but too many times, we miss those opportunities because we are afraid to look.

Part of changing your mindset means accepting that taking leaps is critical to your success. The unknown is a place that allows you to grow and really craft your vision for your life. Fear is what keeps us in one place, holding onto things that might not benefit us, but are comforting because of their familiarity.

Think about it this way. If you know how to achieve a result using one process, you are likely to continue to use that process. However, if that process doesn't work as well as you like, you might explore other options and open yourself up to the idea of trying something different.

While that might work in the processes you complete at work, when it comes to taking greater risks in your professional and personal lives, there is a tendency to do the opposite. We tend to focus on dealing with the broken process, instead of trying to find an alternative and exploring other opportunities.

On the other hand, when I opened my mind up to the possibilities, I also unlocked my potential to create the life I had envisioned for myself. Therefore, be willing to be open to the possibilities. Do not lock yourself into one way of thinking, thus creating tunnel vision regarding what you are capable of accomplishing.

Even if the way that you are doing things has been successful in the past, you need to remember that life is not black and white. There is more than one way to skin a deer. What works successfully for one individual might not work as well for you. Don't be quick to lock yourself into one way of doing things, and thus be unwilling to consider other options.

Our world and society are geared to locking you into a position or a way of thinking, and then discourage you from taking the chance to make a change. Yet, those who have been the most successful, the ones who have created real shifts in how our world functions, started out by taking risks, breaking out of the expectations that had been put on them.

It is helping people create that change and break out of their expectations that inspired me to start a business with my partner, William, to assist aspiring entrepreneurs to be successful as they embark on the path of starting and building a business. At the same time, I have explored the possibilities of real estate investing, built a business using network marketing, and now have become a published author and one day a speaker that will inspire countless of First Nations people around the world. You can create that type of change in your life too! You just have to be willing to stop worrying about what people will think of you. Succeed or not, it's your life. Do what's best for YOU.

It involves breaking out of the box, taking a risk, and then reaping the rewards from stepping onto the path less traveled.

UNDERSTANDING THE EXPECTATIONS THAT KEEP YOU LOCKED IN

A part of any society is the fact that expectations are built into how we are shaped. Cultures include specific events to mark our passage into adulthood. From our courtships through the building of our families, certain expectations are put into place for all of us, based on where we grow up and how we are raised. What can happen, however, is that those expectations can end up being roadblocks that keep us from moving forward and tapping our full potential.

In my childhood, there were multiple roadblocks; circumstances that could have kept me stuck on a path that left me feeling unfulfilled and unable to care for my daughter in a way that I wanted to. I could have continued the cycle of drug dealing and dysfunction, but I decided to strike out into the unknown. You have the power to do the same!

Therefore, I want you to think about the expectations that are part of your life. Are they serving you now or are they blocking you from moving forward? The biggest problem for my people is that the expectations are often set too low and our resources are often limited, and we are left with assumptions that we are not capable or worthy of more than a life of depression and struggles, filled with drug and alcohol abuse.

However, I know that there is more out there for all of us. It starts with a willingness to act on our own behalf, not waiting for someone else to do it for us. We must lose that sense of entitlement because nobody owes us anything. It's up to us to put forth the work that is needed to achieve what we want in life.

Every belief and value you have contributes to the decisions you make, and how you choose to act. Those beliefs and values can be altered as you experience different events throughout your life. Now you can choose to take those experiences and allow them to help you sift through those values and beliefs.

Do you regularly take the time to examine your values and beliefs? Do you ever ask yourself why you believe what you do, or why you value one thing over another? The reason it is important to do so is because you are going to make automatic decisions that impact your future based on those beliefs and values. Shouldn't they reflect who you are now instead of who you used to be?

Recognize that, whether you want to or not, you are constantly being exposed to influences that are changing and shaping you. How are you responding to this shaping? Many of us don't even consciously recognize how we are being altered by these forces, but once you are conscious of how these influences are impacting you, you can choose to accept or reject them. Take this for an example: McDonalds has their advertising everywhere. Literally globally. Everywhere you look, whether it's a billboard, on social media or television. Advertising for their new promotional meal or drink is constantly being programmed into your brain, so when you are hungry or thirsty you subconsciously have the thought of the new stuff instantly pop up in your head. This is all brainwash. The same goes for anything you allow into your brain, even a daily dose of inspiration. So be cautious of what you allow in and choose wisely.

Part of the importance of recognizing these influences is that many of them can keep you in a state of denial about the possibilities in your life. Others could be trying to keep you safe, so they discourage you from taking what they believe to be unnecessary chances. Still others are just negative in general and will tend to bring up everything that could go wrong, every potential obstacle, and even attack your intelligence for thinking about giving it a try.

Notice that those influencers in your circle are fundamentally trying to block you from taking a path that they may have decided not to walk themselves. They truly believe that if a course of action wasn't a fit for them, then it is not a fit for you. It is often the way that our communities, including family and close friends, try to keep us in their circle, but it also leaves many of us trapped in a life that does not benefit us, or allow us to fulfill our potential.

I am here to tell you that it is possible to create a life that you are excited about, one where you can take risks that bring you greater rewards. My life is altered, and I am excited about the future because I opened my mind to the possibilities beyond operating heavy machinery. Now, I am an example to my daughter about pursuing her dreams, regardless of where they take her.

As you shift your mindset, choosing to buck the beliefs of others, you are going to find that you repel those that continue to have a negative frame of mind and start to attract those with a positive and open mindset.

Throughout my journey, I have made decisions based on what inspires and motivates me, not on a fear that I need to get back to work. I am not counting the days until I need to report back to work or let them know that I am not coming back. Instead, I am enjoying this adventure. I am excited to see where it leads me because I know, even though I am not there yet, I am closer than when I first started.

You cannot let fears, especially those of a financial kind, keep you from taking leaps. So many of the inspirational individuals in our world took leaps without a financial safety net. They didn't have an emergency fund or a set date when they would no longer pursue a goal if they weren't successful. They believed in acting to achieve their goals, no matter what financial challenges came their way. An unshakable desire to success. They adapted WIT in their lives, which stands for "WHATEVER IT TAKES."

I want you to take on a mentality that allows you to focus on achieving your goals and overcoming the challenges involved. When you give everything to your efforts, you will see them come to fruition. It starts with recognizing that the people you surround yourself with are going to push you to try harder and go further, or they will focus on trying to pull you down and break your spirit.

CREATE THE CIRCLE THAT SUPPORTS AND INSPIRES

The reason that I want to talk with you about the people you spend time with is that they are going to be part of those forces that influence you for good or bad. If you have specific goals that you want to achieve in life, then you need to surround yourself with those that will support you working to achieve those goals, while at the same time holding you accountable when you are working contrary to what you want to accomplish.

In the years since I moved to the mainland, I met someone who proved to be my biggest supporter and best friend, my dear love Amanda. As my significant other, she has the most influence in my world. If she had tried to stop me from pursuing my dreams, it might have meant the end of my journey. Instead, Amanda chose to step out in faith with me.

Without her, I do not believe I could have accomplished so much, so quickly. She stood by my side, took the leap with me, and our lives continue to blossom. She inspires me to never give up. I have found that surrounding myself with people who push me to be better and take chances are going to give me the fuel necessary to keep going, despite the challenges.

If you spend time with individuals that are not supportive, eventually you will give up. Your goals and dreams will remain unfulfilled and, years later, you will find yourself with regrets over what you should have done, instead of a sense of joy and accomplishment for what you have done. Remember, it is all about the influences that you allow in your life. Studies have shown that we become like the people that we spend the most time with. Who do you spend time with, and whose thoughts and ideas are you being exposed to on a regular basis? Do you have someone that you just know is in your corner that you are confident is adding value to your life?

It is easy to quit when you feel like you have no one in your corner. Amanda and I have been through many tough times, but the point is that we continue to stand together. You need to build that same type of support system, but also be willing to be that support system for others.

I want you to start focusing on how the people around you talk and act. Are they taking risks and inspiring others to follow their dreams? If not, you could be surrounding yourself with naysayers, those who are more likely to try to tear you down than build you up. If you want to make a change in your life, you need to first change your mindset, and then change who you spend your time with. After all, if you are changing your mindset, you need to spend time with individuals who will help you to reinforce that change.

Part of the way that I help myself to stay focused on a new open mindset is by choosing mentors that inspire me and give me critical food for thought. They help me to set my mind up for success. It is not about abandoning who I am, but recognizing that there is more to learn, to do, and more ways to grow as an individual who contributes to my culture and traditions. I also realized that they helped to set up my mindset to take even greater leaps and enjoy the opportunities that are available. It is not about the money, but about the fulfillment that comes from inspiring and being a role model for others from my community.

I choose to surround myself with mentors and associates that respect where I have come from, but who also challenge me to go further and to explore what the world has to offer. I want to leave a legacy for my family, but also to my people. I want them to recognize what is possible for ourselves and our nations. If you believe in yourself, you can achieve a lot in a short period of time, with or without a college education.

If you feel as if the darkness of life is overtaking you, I want you to stop and take an inventory of who you are surrounded by, and what type of encouragement they provide. You might find that they are taking light away and making the darkness appear that much worse.

The world is growing and changing constantly. We all have the wisdom born from our experiences, knowledge, and skills. Part of what makes us rich as human beings is the passing of that wisdom to others. When you find a mentor, you are finding a source of wisdom that you can tap into for your own benefit, and the benefit of those around you.

Start by looking for those that inspire you and then finding ways to interact with them. It could be through their writings or even their speeches. Use that inspiration to help motivate you to act. When you work with a mentor, you will find that you are pulled into their circle, and that will allow you to grow your circle with like-minded individuals who will help you to make the necessary changes to achieve your dreams.

I made some dramatic changes this past year, but much of that work started earlier. When I opened my mind to alternatives beyond the world I was living in, I started to believe I could act and create real change in my life. I saw the possibilities, and it was an exciting time. Still, I admit to having some fear and trepidation about whether I should actually move forward and take this leap into the unknown.

This is where your circle is so important. They will provide encouragement during those times of doubt, and when you wonder if you are truly capable of doing everything that you have ever imagined. Amanda provides that encouragement for me, and I like to think that I am just as supportive of her dreams. It is not a one-way street, but one built on mutual support.

Doubt is the enemy of those who want to build a different life, who see their purpose on a path that is not traditionally followed by those around them. You have the capacity to fight against that doubt by fueling yourself with positive thinking and gathering the tools you need to act.

What are some of those tools?

THE TOOLS THAT CAN INSPIRE YOU TO CREATE

I have already spoken about how important it is to create a circle that supports, encourages, and holds you accountable to create real change. This includes finding mentors and inspiring figures. You do not have to feel limited to just one mentor at a time. Mentors can be part of all aspects of your life, both personal and professional.

Depending on what you want to achieve, you may look for a specific type of mentor who has already walked that path. Over time, you may find yourself choosing another mentor because you have achieved your first goal and are now focused on another aspect of what you want to achieve, which requires help from another individual with experience and skills in that area.

My mentors were chosen because what they said inspired me, motivated me, and gave me food for thought. Remember, my world experience was fairly limited before I started down this path of life. Yet, once I got started, it helped me to reassess my life and understand that nothing was truly out of reach. I just had to act.

Another important tool is to find a means to keep yourself centered on your goals and objectives. The world has a way of naturally distracting us from our goals and objectives, simply because we are presented with challenging circumstances that can appear out of our control. Therefore, it is important to find ways to allow your mind to quiet, thus giving you the opportunity to refocus.

There are a variety of ways to do this. I know some individuals find that peace and clarity when they take the time to exercise daily. Others prefer meditation, taking the time out of the morning and evening to clear their minds through breathing exercises or other forms of meditation. Still others prefer time in nature, where they can reconnect with the air, soil, and animals that are part of our home.

Whatever your preferred method, I want you to make it a regular part of your routine. You can focus on the vision of your achievements, giving them life and very clear details. The point is to make them as rich as possible to make them as real as possible. When you focus on visualizing yourself successful in achieving your goals and endeavors, you will empower yourself to create. You can see yourself acting in a way to reach those goals, which serves as the inspiration to keep you moving forward.

Athletes use visualization techniques all the time to achieve their goals. Doing so, those athletes are inspired to keep up the thoughts and actions that will allow them to do what they want and achieve their goals. They have created a mindset that gives them the ability to be successful, no matter what challenges might come their way.

I find that visualization helps me to manifest my dreams and goals into my reality. The richer the detail, the sharper the image, the faster I can make it happen. Discussing these ideas and dreams with my partner also helps me to see it clearly in my mind. Ask yourself questions to help you flesh out all the details.

Our ancestors often gathered for ceremonies that allowed them to make decisions which guided their course. It was early visualization, and I want you to tap into that. No matter where we are from or how we were raised, we all have the power to create inside of us. Our connection with each other and the earth is what allows us to find success, regardless of the challenges that come our way.

We all have encountered mental quicksand in our lives. It comes in many forms, but we need to be vigilant in looking out for it and avoiding it wherever possible. If you find that you have fallen into a quicksand trap, then you need to stop for a moment, allowing yourself time to reset your mindset back on the path you want to take.

Those resets are not easy, but they can be done with mindful and conscious effort. Do not be quick to assume that just because you were distracted or pulled into that mental quicksand that you cannot pull yourself up and move forward. The fact of the matter is that you will have moments where you fall, where you feel doubt, and where you wonder if you really can be successful. I want you to recognize that when those moments come, you need to walk through them.

It will not always be easy, but it is necessary that you make a conscious effort to do so. It will help you to grow stronger and also give you the endurance necessary to achieve anything you want in life.

When I took my leave of absence, I truly did not know what was going to happen next. However, I left myself open to whatever possibilities presented themselves. Essentially, you have to train yourself not to immediately say no, but be willing to say yes, no matter how crazy or ill-prepared you might feel for the situation. I had to open my mind to the possibilities and be open to exploring what the world had to offer, without fear.

I believe that what you want to achieve in life, you have the power to attract. The universe will give to you what you focus on. If you focus on the positive aspects of a situation and the possibilities available to you, you will draw more opportunities to yourself. A path you might never have embarked on will open up right in front of you. It is this power that you need to tap to create a real directional shift in where your life is headed.

One of the effects of creating change for yourself is that you end up being able to impact others. After all, you do not live in a vacuum. While others are influencing you, you are influencing others.

Think of how great speakers can get you to think differently, can inspire you to act differently, and can chart a different course for various institutions. I want you to recognize that you have the same power within you. We all do!

I want you to be inspired to see the valuable person that you are and use that vision to create and build a future that can be a guidepost to others. There are so many ways to impact others. Like a ripple in a pond, those efforts can spread farther than you ever imagined! Here are just a few of the ones that can give others a jolt of inspiration and leave you with joy and love in your heart.

Volunteer – Do you know how many organizations need volunteers to achieve their missions? You could work with young people, old people, people who have been dealt horrible circumstances, those struggling to overcome an addiction to drugs or alcohol, and so much more. You have the power to influence their lives for the better, just by your presence and a willingness to listen. Always remember that whatever inspires you, there is likely an organization trying to move that agenda forward. Take part and recognize the gift you give when you give of yourself!

Invest – I am not just talking about finding the right financial investments. I mean invest in people. Be kind, be willing to forgive, and be willing to lend a hand. When we invest in each other, then we can create large-scale change. Jesus Christ is credited with saying there is more happiness in giving than in receiving. Give to others and see how it benefits your mindset and inspires you to keep those investments going.

Mentor – I also want you to recognize that you can serve as a mentor to others. It is a gift that keeps on giving, one that can allow you to pass down your wisdom to others. Mentoring is not a top-down affair. Someone that you mentor can also inspire you as well. Be open to the possibilities and you can truly be a gift to another individual looking to create change in their life.

As you can see, my life is in motion right now. I am writing, investing, and creating the life that I want, one that will allow me to care for my family and pursue those items on my bucket list. I chose to move away from a dark path based on the past choices of myself and others to create one that is filled with light and laughter. You don't have to be chained down to a way of living that leaves with a lifetime of regrets. Instead, I want you to focus on what is possible and then make it a reality.

There is no vision that is too great or too small for you to achieve. The biggest obstacle that you will ever have in your life is the one that you create by means of your mindset. When you choose a positive mindset, you are blasting that obstacle out of the water. Do not see risk as something to avoid, but rather as a means to achieve even more in your life.

I want to inspire you and help you to move forward in creating dramatic change in your life. I am always available via social media, and for those who know me, feel free to see how we can work together, how I can serve as a mentor, or even just share with you what inspires me to get out of bed and keep my focus.

I hope that you recognize that the darkness in your life does not have to win. You can let in the light and achieve more than you might have dreamed was possible. For those that need a boost, see my story as one that you can create for yourself. Recognize that I am just getting started. Your willingness to pick up this book means that you are ready to take a leap, and are just looking for the motivation. I hope I have provided that! May the life you want be manifested in your reality, and may you tap into your creative abilities.

"Use Your Struggles Today As Motivation For Tomorrow"

— Kirk Jakesta

Please visit Kirk Jakesta's website for more information, www.StreamLineToSuccess.com

Never Give Up!

My Journey to Purpose

VIVIAN STARK

NEVER GIVE UP: GROWTH AND SUCCESS COME IN INCREMENTS, NOT LEAPS

My desire is to encourage you with my life story. I have spent my life learning and improving myself, and I am thrilled to share what I have learned with you. Today I am living my definition of success. I have said NO TO THE PITY PARTY! Personal growth and development are a daily diet staple, and have fueled me in my business and entrepreneurial successes.

I wake up every day, knowing I am living my life with purpose, knowing I am the kind of person I always wanted to be. I have faced many challenges; my story has failures as well as successes. But I have learned that setbacks are only a part of the story; they are not the whole story. The story keeps going as long as you keep trying. You can choose to quit and make the story end in failure or dissatisfaction, or you can choose to keep trying and make your story what you want it to be.

Never give up. Success and growth do not come in leaps, they come in increments. The challenges will keep coming at you and sometimes it feels like two steps forward, one step back. But remember you did have those steps forward and you will again – if you never give up. You can choose to be overcome by dreck that life throws at you, or you can open your eyes to the love and opportunity that are always there too. You can have the life you want if you never, never, never give up on what is important – You.

IT IS YOUR LIFE - LIVE IT YOUR WAY

My life is my own for the making, but I did not always know this. I lived a very sheltered life as a child, fiercely protected by my overbearing Greek parents. I was not allowed to do the 'normal' girl things, like have sleepovers or join the Girl Guides to be a Brownie. When I was older I was not allowed to date for fear of gossip within my community. My parents lived in fear of the unknown. I lived in fear of being reprimanded if I disobeyed.

Despite my fear, insecurity, and extremely introverted personality, I pushed myself to exert my independence and fulfill certain goals that I set out for myself. From a very young age, I felt that I always needed to prove myself. To prove that I was pretty enough, smart enough, or even good enough. I worked tirelessly to achieve my dreams, never sharing them with anyone for fear of being ridiculed.

I began pursuing my goals as a young teen who wanted to fit in. I lived in an affluent area of Vancouver and always felt out of place. I did not have all the cool clothes that everyone else had, so I worked with my brother as a gardener cutting grass for one of my dad's clients. I saved my money and bought the clothes I wanted so that I would 'fit in' with the crowd. Despite this, I never felt that I fit in with other kids.

I was a rather "ugly duckling" as a younger girl, with a massive overbite and awkward shyness about me. After having braces, I felt my "ugly" stage was behind me and I decided to take a modeling class over several weeks one summer when I was in high school. My parents did not support me in this decision, so I chose to pay for it myself. The modeling class cost $800. I worked at Zellers for $3.00/hour. I persevered and saved enough money to pay for the class.

It turns out that the modeling class was just what I needed. I learned how to carry myself and exude confidence. After finishing the class, I took several modeling jobs and had many successes in my short modeling career. I made the cover of the then prestigious Back to School catalog for Eaton's Department Store, along with several other fun and exciting modeling adventures.

My modeling highlight and a fond memory was when I was hired for a ski catalog. (They wanted a curvy model. Who knew that sometimes it pays to not be super skinny!) We were taken up to the top of Blackcomb Mountain by helicopter before the official ski season opening. I remember having to jump out of the helicopter into three feet of snow because the helipad was snow-covered, and the helicopter could not land. I was paid $850 per day for three days. It was a dream come true. I felt validated.

When I was nineteen I began dating a handsome Greek guy I met at a wedding. Before I knew it, his parents and my parents got together and began planning our wedding. I literally cannot remember him actually asking me to marry him. How sad is that? Some time before our wedding I found out that he was into drugs and was still seeing his ex-girlfriend. I broke up with him and cancelled the wedding.

To escape well-meaning friends and relatives, I took an extended holiday to Greece where I could recover from the breakup. Armed with my modeling composite cards and my lovely, fashionable clothes, I hoped to land some modeling jobs while I was there. Instead, I met another handsome Greek guy who was smooth and charming. He swept me off my feet.

In classic old-school Greek fashion, my mom flew to Greece to check him out and determine whether he was a suitable partner for me. Like I said, I lived a sheltered life. She approved and, after a civil wedding in Canada, I moved to Greece to start my life with my new husband.

The first thing he did when we settled in to our home was give away all my beloved clothes. He proceeded to tell me what I could and could not do, where I could and could not go, and how I had to act. He, like my parents, was consumed with what other people thought of him and now me. I was terrified. What had I done?

I realized very quickly I had made a huge mistake and wanted to leave him and go back to Canada. To my surprise, I was already pregnant. Too embarrassed to tell anyone my sad state of affairs, I stayed in Greece. I had made an agreement with my husband that our children would be born in Canada. I did not want to risk my children having to go to the army if they were boys. After my first son was born, I returned to Greece.

When I became pregnant with my second son, I decided to leave Greece, not to return. I told my husband I was going back to Canada and he could come with me or not. He chose to move to Canada with me, but we broke up after a few years. Our marriage was just not meant to be, but I was blessed with two healthy, adorable and rambunctious boys that I loved so much.

Once divorced, my husband went back to Greece to avoid paying child support and to be near his momma, so she could pamper and take care of him. (It's a Greek thing. He was a huge momma's boy. Never again.) I was determined that my two boys would never be momma's boys!

THE SETBACK IS NOT THE END OF THE STORY
PUSH YOURSELF TO YOUR NEXT GREAT CHAPTER

For the next few years, I lived in low-income housing while raising my boys and working at Woodward's department store. Then, I left my job at Woodward's and began a career in banking. I started out on the front lines working as a teller. After six weeks I was promoted to the prestigious side counter position. Within a year I was promoted again to managing tens of millions of dollars of lawyers' trust funds in an exclusive, independent position.

I was always pushing myself to be better, to do more, be more, have more so I could give more. I wanted to improve myself and my income to support my family. I had an internal drive to never give up. I wanted to prove everyone wrong. I would make it. I could do this! During these years I learned to appreciate life's lessons and gifts and I continued to grow.

Ten years after my first marriage, I married a second time. I became pregnant soon after our wedding in Hawaii but spent most of my time during our marriage being neglected by my husband. As soon as my daughter was born, I no longer existed in his eyes. I later found out that my husband had a girlfriend before, during, and after our entire marriage. He worked with her; she was married, too, and the four of us occasionally hung out together as couples. Needless to say, the marriage did not last, but I would not change a thing as I have my beautiful daughter from that relationship.

I spent the next years relentlessly trying to find my passion. I worked in banking, direct sales, office supplies, a genealogical search company, and as a sales manager for a roofing distribution company. I also went to night school while working full-time and raising my kids, to get my diploma in International Trade. Additionally, I began a calling card company in Santiago, Chile that I launched at the Canada/Chile Trade Mission in 2003.

OPPORTUNITY KEEPS KNOCKING, SO OPEN THE DOOR!

I was very proud of the calling card company. It was a crazy dream, but I wanted to make it happen. Recognizing a huge opportunity, I wanted to offer an affordable service that we took for granted in Canada. The large telecommunications companies had a very different view on my entry to the marketplace and I was forced out of business when they pressured my distribution channel to drop me. Unfortunately, my venture was short-lived after significant effort and money had been invested. I planned to travel back to Chile to negotiate a deal with another distributor when I was rear-ended in a car accident and suffered severe whiplash, leaving me unable to travel. I had to move on from this company but by this time I knew it was not the end. I knew other opportunities would come my way.

By 2007, I was working for a computer company selling proprietary software and hardware for restaurants. My expertise in sales and customer service had grown significantly by then. I had come a long way from the introverted little Greek girl who thought she was not good enough. With perseverance, training, and a belief in myself I had become a great salesperson.

I loved working with customers and was enjoying my new career when I began having severe migraines regularly. I was also having issues with my sinuses. I thought I probably had a severe sinus infection, but my nose and upper gums were numb, which was troubling.

That August was one big headache, literally. I had eight migraines that month and each one put me down for two to five days. I went to the doctor and had several tests run, including a CT scan. After the CT scan doctors finally determined the cause of my sinus trouble and migraines.

I will never forget that day. The doctor's office called and scheduled me for a 7:00 PM appointment. The doctor came in and told me that I had a brain tumor and that she was very sorry, but she did not know whether it was benign or malignant. She had not consulted a neurologist before meeting with me. I drove home in a state of shock and called my mom to tell her the news.

I learned that I had a meningioma, a benign brain tumor. After an MRI, I learned it measured 3.3 x 3.4 x 4.4 cm, was in my right frontal lobe, and had probably been growing for twenty or thirty years. Only recently had it grown large enough to begin causing migraines, sinus pain, and facial numbness.

Within a month I would be having major brain surgery to remove the tumor. Oddly enough, I was not scared until the day of the surgery, when it really sunk in. I had been told that the tumor was in an excellent location for surgery and that I would not need chemo or radiation afterwards. The tumor was not going to kill me. But with any surgery there is always a risk.

I do not remember much that happened the first week or so post-surgery. When I really came around and began noticing things, the first thing that caught my attention was that I was having significant vision problems. The brain surgeon had touched a nerve in my right eye, causing fourth nerve palsy. I always had this weird talent to do crazy thing with my eyes and move them independently, but this was something I could not control. I had severe double vision. I could only see straight when I looked through a very narrow view if I tilted my chin down. And I could not look to my left at all. When I tried, I lost all focus and control of my eyes.

This condition is similar to a child having a wandering eye. Actually, I had to be seen at Vancouver Children's Hospital to have my condition monitored. This was a very challenging time for me. It was one of the worst times of my life. I had so much stress and anxiety wondering if my vision would be like this forever. My head was permanently disfigured, leaving my self-esteem at an all-time low. My jaw was so stiff from surgery that I could barely open my mouth to eat. I was house-bound, and unable to walk up or down stairs without assistance. I could not read or watch TV to occupy myself because I was constantly dizzy. Every negative thought you could possibly imagine ran through my mind thousands of times each day. I wish I had known then what I know now about keeping a positive mindset, the healing powers of affirmations, an attitude of gratitude, and the law of attraction.

I cannot stress enough how important it is to reach out to family and friends to help you during a medical crisis (or any crisis, for that matter). Having people who love you to support you is so important. Being the independent person that I am, I did not ask for much help. Silly me. Stupid me, actually. I did not want to worry my kids any more than they already were. My mother was such an angel. She lived nearby and prepared meals for us, but for the most part, I was alone in my thoughts in a very dark place.

About five weeks into my recovery, I met someone online. Bored out of my mind, I had gone on a dating site, half-blind, looking for strangers to converse with me. Talk about being desperate! For our first meeting, I rode the bus to downtown Vancouver where we met for a drink. He must have thought I was rather forward on a first date when I grabbed his arm to walk up a few stairs. Little did he know that I grabbed his arm so that I would not fall flat on my face.

We hit it off and developed a relationship. He picked me up every day for several weeks and took me out on his random errands just to get me out of the house. Sometimes we would just hang out. At first, I only told him that I'd had a recent eye surgery. Eventually I told him the extent of the surgery. He was also having some challenges in his life, so it was wonderful to be able to help each other. I cannot tell you what a godsend he was for me. He came into my life exactly when I needed him, and I am forever grateful for what he did for me.

Worried about losing my job, I returned to work twelve weeks post-surgery. I was worried about paying my bills and the mortgage on the house I had recently purchased. I needed the money, or so I thought. In hindsight, that was the worst decision I could have made. I suffered with migraines and vision issues for several weeks before the universe decided I'd had enough. All of the senior managers, including me, were laid off from our jobs. It was the biggest blessing.

I did not work for two years. It was a very trying time. The line of credit was on a steady increase as the months went by, but I needed to heal. My vision took over a year to somewhat normalize, and the severe numbness in my face post surgery lasted for several years.

During this period, I had a lot of time to think. My surgery was a life-changing experience. I could have died. I decided to take on a totally different view on life from this time forward. From this point on, any time an opportunity presented itself I was going to take it.

DEFINE YOUR WORK AND WHAT YOU NEED

Knowing that after all my health problems I would need a job that allowed me to make my health a priority, I decided to choose a job that would work for me rather than choosing to work for the job. I started slowly by taking a 100% sales commission, part-time position that allowed me to work as much or as little as I wanted.

I told my bosses about my medical condition, and that I was not sure how I would respond to being back to work. My boss told me that as long as I was meeting or exceeding my quotas that he would not micromanage me. I would be allowed to do my own thing, which was perfect for me. For some this would be a scary venture to undertake, but I was up for the challenge.

I pushed myself by working long hours, often answering customer emails at 6:00 AM before I went to work and again well into the evening. I needed to build up my customer base and wanted to ensure they were well taken care of. Within less than six months I was working full-time and making a full-time income. I was back!

After working for this company for about four years, a couple of millennials were hired into the mix, and that changed everything for me. I was working independently with little interaction with my bosses for the most part and the millennials were cc'ing him on every email they sent. This is when my interest in generational differences in the workplace was first piqued.

Although I enjoyed the work and my co-workers, my bosses were a different story. My work environment left much to be desired. Receiving year-end bonuses based on sales is a standard practice in the world of sales. When I did not receive a bonus at the end of 2013 because my boss said I was "already making too much money," I decided to look at other business opportunities. Forever the entrepreneur!

I continued working my sales job while seeking other opportunities. I joined an Australian direct sales company and quickly rose to the top of their company, becoming one of their top 20 earners out of 20,000 consultants. I had 1,700 consultants on my team and was the only director in North America. I earned free trips to Australia, Dubai, Aruba, Florence, Manchester, Dallas, and Los Angeles. I finally left my sales job in 2016 to pursue my new business venture full-time.

DREAM BIG AND HELP OTHERS DREAM TOO

I LOVED working with my team. Coaching and mentoring were my passion. In October 2016, I attended a One Day to Greatness seminar with Jack Canfield in Kamloops, BC. After a brief conversation with Jack, I decided to take his Train the Trainer course to become a certified Success Principles Trainer. The intention was to share this new knowledge with my team. I had found purpose and passion in supporting others to build successful teams. I felt fulfilled when I saw their self-esteem and confidence grow. They were conquering their fears and winning!

Unfortunately, I had to resign from the direct sales company in February 2017 when they started having issues with production and delivery. Later that year the company declared bankruptcy. I went through a lot of stress, anxiety, and loss of sleep. Panic attacks became the daily norm for me. I had known the CEO for over eighteen years and was completely in the dark about the state of the company. My team was upset and blaming me. I received a constant stream of Facebook messages and harassing emails. The downfall of the company was out of my control, so I had to bow out. But this was not my first time at the rodeo. I knew that my story did not stop here if I chose to keep trying.

I met someone in late 2016 who introduced me to an opportunity to speak and train businesses on generational differences in the workplace. I was fascinated by this as I saw the struggles my own millennial children were having at work. I look back now at the communication challenges that existed in my previous jobs and wish I knew then how the different generations think and process information. I wanted to more closely understand their environment and what I could do to help. It made perfect sense that bridging the generation gap would improve productivity, communication, collaboration, and make for a happier, more cohesive work environment.

I now know that the behaviors, attitudes, beliefs, experiences, and influences during an individual's formative years really shape who they are and how they behave in all areas of their lives. I was excited about my new-found knowledge, and planned to launch my speaking business by mid-2017.

I hired an image consultant to come to my home and do a complete wardrobe change to prepare me for my speaking career. Having someone go through my wardrobe and tell me to get rid of most of it was a very difficult experience. There were a few tears. I must have attachment issues! I eventually embraced the change and spent thousands of dollars on a new wardrobe to complete my new look.

Then, as luck would have it, I broke a veneer on my front tooth. No big deal, I thought. I had been through this before and would just have it replaced.

This was the beginning of my dental nightmare. From May 31, 2017 through December 21, 2017, I had twenty-six dental appointments to fix my front tooth. I began lisping and developed what doctors believe is a stress-related condition. I lost the saliva in my mouth, had burning in my throat from acid reflux brought on by stress, my voice was constantly hoarse, and I spent several months waking up with panic attacks. I never knew from one to day to the next if I would have a voice or not, so I had to put everything on hold.

I saw every doctor and specialist I believed might be able to help me. I was taking six pills a day to help with my various symptoms. I hated this! I needed to feel better; I needed to heal my body naturally. I would not stop until I got the answers I needed. I moved away from traditional medicine, stopped taking all my medications, and began incorporating EFT (Emotional Freedom Technique), also known as Tapping, Reiki, and Bioenergy work, to heal my body.

Eventually, my body and voice were getting to the point where I could speak relatively well, I decided to move forward with the training business. I hired a business coach to get me on the right track, mentally and physically. He helped me tremendously during a very difficult time. I also attended Raymond Aaron's Speaker and Communication Workshop, which totally changed my training and speaking style. It gave me the confidence I was lacking and sent me on a whole new trajectory for my business. I began my own company, Gen-Connect Training in early 2018. It has been an amazing ride. I am much more at peace and ready for the next stage in my life.

LIVING IN THE POSITIVE HAS MADE MY LIFE

Although I have been blessed with many struggles, I have also enjoyed many successes. I have experienced relationships that did not work out, work and business challenges, worries when raising three children as a single parent, medical challenges, and many dreams and goals that seemed impossible. The one thing I always knew for sure was that if I gave up and wallowed in self-pity, I would be letting myself and my children down. That was not an option. Success was the only acceptable outcome.

I wanted to show my children what a strong, self-sufficient and resourceful mother I could be, and that they could always rely on me. I wanted to set an example and prove to myself and my children that I could provide for us no matter what. I am very proud of the amazing people my children have become; they are strong, independent, kind, respectful, and loving. This is the true meaning of success for me. Out of all the things I have accomplished thus far, they are my crowning glory.

FIVE STRATEGIES FOR A SUCCESSFUL LIFE

1) **Always have a positive mindset.** This is a crucial component. Before you get into the power of a positive mindset and the law of attraction, spend some time listening to what you are currently telling yourself. Check in with yourself. What is going on with you? We constantly speak to ourselves with an inner voice which is sometimes quietly whispering and sometimes yelling. Once you have spent a few days noticing how you speak to yourself, you may not like it very much; after all, you are your own worst critic. Be accountable for how you speak to yourself. Never fear, you have the power to change that inner voice!

Do you believe you are the product of everything that has happened to you in your life? Your inner voice may try to convince you that you are a victim of your circumstances and your past. Reflect and acknowledge the things that have happened to you and where you are now. Then prepare to move past them.

2) Shift your mindset using the law of attraction. You can influence things around you so that things happen FOR you rather than TO you. The universal principle of the law of attraction is that 'like attracts like.' The law of attraction manifests through your thoughts by drawing to you not only thoughts and ideas that are alike, but also people who think like you, along with corresponding situations and possibilities. It is the magnetic power of the universe which draws similar energies to each other.

The law of attraction is already working in your life, intentional or not. If you have a negative mindset, many unpleasant or unwanted things are probably happening in your life, and you may see negative things happening all around you. Think back to how you speak to yourself. Be mindful of your thoughts and that inner voice. Begin to think positively.

Along with thinking positively, begin to intentionally think and feel the things that you would like to have in your life. The most common things people desire are love, a career, good relationships, health, and wealth. Visualize a mental image of what you want to achieve. Repeat positive, affirming statements to create and bring into your life what you visualize or repeat in your mind. In other words, use the power of your thoughts and words.

Imagine that what you desire is already a part of your life. Acknowledge it with each of your five senses, to the extent that you can. Spend time imagining your life once you have acquired what it is that you want. Write out your affirmations and read them aloud at least once daily. You will begin to draw them to you when you act as though you already have what it is that you want. Persistence is key!

3) Take calculated risks. Do you encourage yourself to stay where you are and play it safe? Safe can be dangerous. I encourage you to take calculated risks. If you do not try new things you will never know how far you can go. When opportunities present themselves, jump on them. It may be your one and only chance. Push yourself and do not take no for an answer. Keep digging until you find the answer you want.

Quitting is always an option. Well, it is an option for those who are content living a mediocre life. Quitting is an option unless you want to live an amazing life with a purpose. If you want to live the life of your dreams, you must not give up. Do not give up and never stop learning. If you continue to learn, you will continue to grow both personally and professionally.

4) Appreciate all of life's lessons and gifts with an attitude of gratitude. Learn and grow from your failures. Let life's challenges teach you to persevere even when all you want to do is give up. Remind yourself that the only outcome you will accept is success.

5) NEVER Give Up. We all face adversities and challenges in life. It takes character, drive, and a positive mindset to persevere, overcome, and excel in life. The only person who can stop you from achieving your goals is you. If I can do it, so can you. Go for it!

Do you, your team, or organization want to be inspired to change your future and find your purpose?

Do you want to learn how mastering the Five Strategies for a Successful Life can empower you in both your personal and professional career?

Do you want to say "NO TO THE PITY PARTY" and achieve the life you truly desire?

Vivian Stark is an inspirational speaker and corporate trainer living in Vancouver, B.C. Canada, whose captivating story will inspire you to live the life you want if you never, never, never give up on what's important – You.

As a generational and workplace effectiveness expert, Vivian's career centers around helping others work in a more collaborative and cohesive work environment. Her focus on engagement and accountability both in and outside of the workplace mirrors her personal belief of how you must take 100% responsibility in all areas of your life. Learn how giving up blaming, complaining and excuse making can lead you to live a life filled with peace, happiness and personal fulfillment.

To learn how you can incorporate her knowledge and expertise into your life and business with ease and confidence, reach out to Vivian at www.gen-connect.ca. Vivian is available for private or corporate speaking engagements.

Motivation Does Activate and Sustain Behaviour

How to Bring Results in Life and Business

JULIE HOGBIN

B efore we talk about motivation in any great detail, it would be a good idea to cover the basics about what motivation really is. There are many, many, theories and huge amounts of research has been conducted on the subject over many decades. To be honest, with all the information out there it can be confusing as to what it all means.

One thing is for sure, one theory — one piece of information — does not cover it all as each researcher has their own bent and interpretation on the subject. It is when you are able to link it all together that it starts to make sense and you are able to do something with the information to help yourself.

I have researched, read about, practiced, and taught this subject to over 20,000 Leaders in Life, Business and the Entrepreneur market, both one-on-one and in small groups for very nearly three decades, and I am still learning.

This chapter is based around my knowledge, my interpretation, and a definition of Motivation that I have worked with for a long time. I have neither found nor developed a better definition — yet!

"Motivation is a conscious or unconscious driving force that arouses and directs action towards the achievement of a desired goal."

ClaimYourDestiny.global   #ConsciousLeadership

So, what does this mean in reality? It means that we are motivated by internal and external factors and that sometimes we know what those factors are and sometimes we don't: Our actions and thoughts are both conscious and unconscious in nature. It also means that the motives provoke a reaction and an action that help us 'get' something we want — a goal — and as a driving force they are powerful.

So my 1st questions to you are:

- What is your goal?

- What are you working towards?

- How many goals do you have?

- What is driving you?

- How conscious are you?

Motivation is an internal force; we are the only ones who can motivate us. Motivation can be affected by external influences. Ultimately it is us, and only us, that make the decision to do or not to do something. Nobody can make you feel or do anything! It is your absolute choice to capitulate and do, or to resist and not do.

We make the decision based on the information we have at the time and how confident we feel. There are many emotions and personal characteristics that come into play when we are talking about motivation and all that entails.

When we say that others motivate us what it really means is that they have created an environment that inspires us to do something. We make the decision out of fear in some cases, because we know it makes sense in other cases, because we aspire to be like the individual, or, more simply, just because we want to.

For you, and everybody else, your desired goal always provides you with a positive outcome. It gives you something you want even if that want is unconsciously driven. For others viewing it from their perspective, that outcome may be viewed as negative.

Let me explain what I mean with a couple of examples.

Addicts of any description do whatever it takes to fuel their need. They are achieving their desired outcome with more alcohol, more food, less food, more drugs, or just more of something, and they will go to extreme lengths to get it, such as selling personal and other people's belongings, lying and deceiving, going into debt and stealing.

Someone comes home with great intent of doing some research, maybe to write a book or to do some personal development such as going to the gym, and they end up sitting in front of the TV for hours with a bottle of wine. What is their driving force? We may not understand it as the viewer but there is definitely one for the person being observed.

Let's look at a couple of positive examples with a more generally accepted encouraging outcome.

A young person decides what they want to achieve in their life. They study like crazy to get the grades required to get to the top university and to study in a class of four with the top professor in their subject matter field, and they achieve it.

An individual from an underprivileged background wants to change their life, achieve greater things than have ever been achieved in their family, and become independently wealthy, and they are successful in achieving their goals.

Now for every example shared the opposite can be true as well. Not everybody becomes an addict, not everyone slouches in front of the TV, not every student achieves their potential, and not every underprivileged individual becomes independently wealthy.

"Everything you do is goal-driven. Everything you do is because you want the end result — whatever that end result may be!"

ClaimYourDestiny.global   #ConsciousLeadership

The examples are all based on how motivated the individual is to achieve their goal. Now if you know your goal consciously, can keep it in focus and resist the temptation of your old ways, you can achieve marvellous results.

The rest of this chapter will look at what drives you and how you can change your habits and behaviours over a period both short and long term, with the aim to achieve whatever it is you want.

I reference no theory in this chapter. There are many to read and learn which are of use to us all intellectually and unless the theory is practically applied and interpreted into reality all they remain are theories. I have spent decades interpreting theories into real life behaviours that make a difference for the better.

A few more questions for you to think about first.

- What are your drivers?

- What are your values?

- What is your risk tolerance?

- How much do you want to fit in with the 'norm' of your social group?

- How much do you really want, on a scale of 1 to 10, the thing it is you are aiming to achieve?

- How comfortable are you with change?

There are a lot more questions to ask but these will start you on the journey to understand your own motivators.

"Your motives create your habits, for good and bad, as they are your driving force."

ClaimYourDestiny.global   #ConsciousLeadership

There is so much information coming at us on a minute by minute basis. We make thousands upon thousands of decisions every day — so many in fact, we cannot be conscious of all the decisions, to do or not to do something, that we do make. We would be completely overwhelmed if we did.

So what do we do? We create patterns of behaviour that we do not have to think about, as it is quicker that way, to achieve our outcomes. We create habits that get us what we want in the easiest manner.

"Your habits have created your behaviour through your values, beliefs, and attitudes."

ClaimYourDestiny.global   #ConsciousLeadership

HABITS

Habits are a set of thoughts, behaviours, and ways of being that are developed through repeated behaviour. Habits are formed from the moment we become aware that there is a 'norm' of how to do things. Some we pick up from our parents, guardians, siblings, and influential individuals around us at a very early age. Others we develop for ourselves through the maturing process.

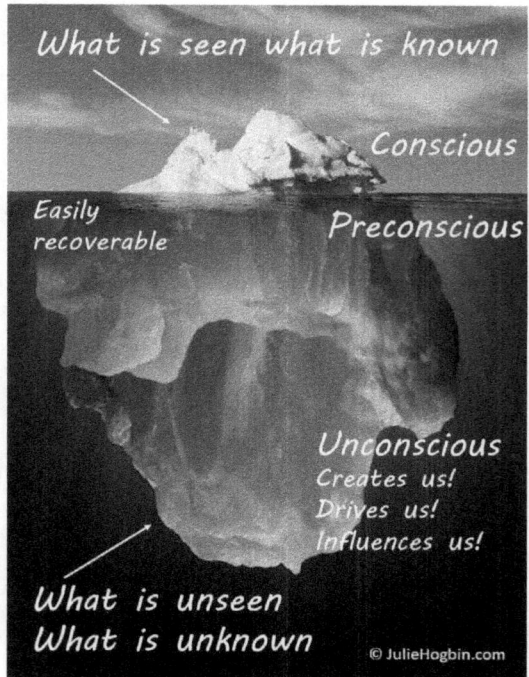

What is seen what is known
Conscious
Easily recoverable
Preconscious
Unconscious
Creates us!
Drives us!
Influences us!
What is unseen
What is unknown
© JulieHogbin.com

"Look to your parents for your beliefs about the world and yourself – you may be amazed at the similarities."

ClaimYourDestiny.global   #ConsciousLeadership

Once habits are created they can be difficult to break. To break a habit, we must consciously think about doing something different and then do it — which can equal hard work and being uncomfortable.

The thing is, we can all break habits if we really want to. BUT (and there is a big BUT) the unconscious part of our being is there to keep us safe. Any change and it may feel we are under threat and revert quickly to the old ways.

"Talk to your unconscious and ask its permission if you want to change some deep held habits and motivations to do things in a new way."

"Sounds a bit weird? Well it works, try it for yourself."

ClaimYourDestiny.global   #ConsciousLeadership

VALUES

Your values are a central part of who you are and who you want to be. By becoming more aware of these driving motivators in your life, you can use them as a guide to make the best choice in any situation.

Your decisions and actions, when in line with your values, will be easy to make and put into practice. If you are attempting to do something that is not held as a value to you, you will find it harder to do and, potentially, you will be in conflict with yourself.

Here is an example. If one of your values is honesty and you are in a relationship, business or personal, with someone who you know tells untruths, how hard will you find it to trust them? What will this do to your behaviour and your motivation within the relationship?

Values can be worked with, reordered, and installed — so do not lose hope. I personally have needed to work hard on my value regarding money. To say the least, it was slightly askew!

ATTITUDES

Your attitude is a predisposition to respond either negatively or positively towards an idea, object, person, or situation. It is the way you feel about something or someone. It can also be a particular feeling or opinion. It is seen as a conscious behaviour but will come from an unconscious driver.

Your attitude evolves as a result of your beliefs and values and will influence:

- Your choice of action and behaviour

- Your response to challenges

- Your response to incentives

- Your response to a word

- Your response to someone trying to help you

We all have an attitude — we cannot not have one. Generally, when it is said someone has an attitude it is meant as a negative opinion, but attitudes are drivers for good as well. It is just a common adaptation of a word which is more often linked to negativity.

As with anything else we do, our attitude is a choice we make. My choice, and I trust yours as you are reading this book, is to start each day with a positive attitude — it soon becomes a habit.

If you want to change something in your life, surround yourself with those who are on the same path or learn from those who have already done the 'thing' that you want to do. Attitudes are contagious so eradicate those personally held by yourself and those that are owned by people that may be in your circle who aren't helping you. If you don't know what your attitudes are, ask someone for feedback who will tell you the truth.

Also carefully study your close associates to make your own decisions on who stays with you on your journey and who leaves, their attitudes can be contagious. Look at the relationships that are in your life and acknowledge whether they are supporting you or hindering you. Decisions then can be made from a realistic position of what you want to do.

SOCIAL INTELLIGENCE

Social intelligence indicates that portions of our knowledge acquisition can be directly related to observing others within the context of social interactions, experiences and media influences.

So what does this mean to all of us? Basically, it means that if we see something that is rewarded, we copy it so that we get rewarded. We achieve the same result as we have observed, therefore we have achieved our result, which was our goal. There is far more to it but that's the basic concept. We learn by example from others.

So who do we copy? We copy those close to us and we adopt behaviours to fit into the crowd and belong. As we get older, we copy those who we admire or those who we aspire to be like. We develop a sense of self and become more aware of what it is we want. We begin to lead rather than follow — well some of us do and I expect you are a leader since you are reading this book! Join my Facebook group for more, https://www.facebook.com/groups/ClaimYourDestiny/

We are motivated to belong to a group with a certain set of characteristics. That could be because it is what we want or it can be because we know no different. It can be through peer pressure or choice, but whichever route we take it is ultimately our choice!

Join my Facebook group for more, https://www.facebook.com/groups/ClaimYourDestiny/

It is these drivers of behaviour that make you act differently from, or the same as, others in any given situation. So, by understanding these drivers, you

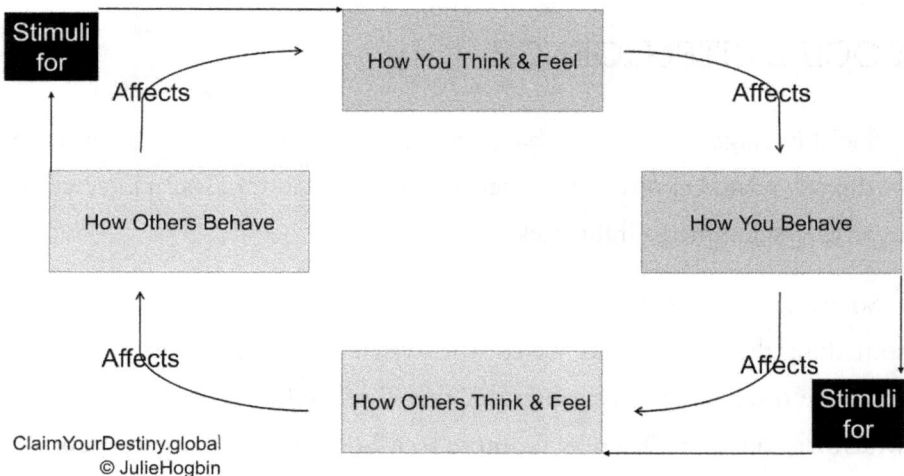

Stimuli for

How You Think & Feel

Affects

Affects

How Others Behave

How You Behave

Affects

How Others Think & Feel

Affects

Stimuli for

ClaimYourDestiny.global
© JulieHogbin

can better understand why you do the things you do. The skill is not only to understand your conscious needs, but also those that are unconscious in nature.

"In the choice between changing one's mind and proving there's no need to do so, most people get busy on the proof."

-John Kenneth Galbraith

SELF-PERCEPTION

Self-perception is the belief or disbelief in our own capabilities to achieve a goal or an outcome. These beliefs provide the foundation for human motivation, well-being, and personal accomplishment. This is because unless you believe that your actions can produce the outcomes you desire, you will have little incentive to act or to persevere in the face of difficulties.

Of course, human functioning is influenced by many factors. The success or failure you experience as you engage the countless tasks that comprise your life naturally influences the many decisions you must make. Also, the knowledge and skills you possess will certainly play critical roles in what you choose to do and not do.

"People's level of motivation, emotional states, and actions are based more on what they believe than on what is objectively true. For this reason, how you behave can often be better predicted by the beliefs you hold about your capabilities than by what you are actually capable of accomplishing."

ClaimYourDestiny.global   #ConsciousLeadership

You only need to watch one of the reality TV shows to see how clearly some people are deluded about their own abilities. The opposite is also true — you talk to someone who you know is gifted and they think and believe the complete opposite.

Our upbringing and early influencers, or even a recent happening, have a huge part to play in how and what we believe about ourselves. The great news though is whatever has happened in the past does not have to happen in our future.

These perceptions help determine what you do with the knowledge and skills you have. They also explain why your behaviours are sometimes not matched to your actual capabilities and why your behaviour may differ widely from somebody else, even when you have similar knowledge and skills.

For example, many talented people suffer frequent (and sometimes debilitating) bouts of self-doubt about capabilities they clearly possess, just as many individuals are confident about what they can accomplish despite possessing a modest repertoire of skills. Belief and reality are seldom perfectly matched, and individuals are typically guided by their beliefs when they engage the world.

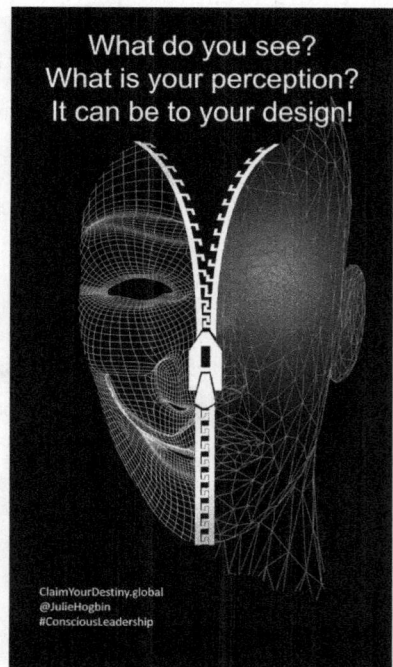

What do you see?
What is your perception?
It can be to your design!

ClaimYourDestiny.global
@JulieHogbin
#ConsciousLeadership

As a consequence, your accomplishments are generally better predicted by your self-perception than by your previous achievements, knowledge, or skills. Of course, no amount of confidence or self-appreciation can produce success when requisite skills and knowledge are absent.

"Skills and knowledge can all be gained if you want them enough and you find the right mentor to teach you."

ClaimYourDestiny.global   #ConsciousLeadership

COLLECTIVE PERCEPTION

Because individuals operate collectively as well as individually, self-perception is both a personal and a social construct. Collective systems develop a sense of collective effectiveness, it can create the group's shared belief in its capability to attain goals and accomplish desired tasks.

One brain is one but the collective brainpower of a group equals more than the sum of its parts — it's the adage $1+1=3$ or $2+2=5$. However, this is only true when the collective works together in harmony with the same aim. If members of the collective are working against each other one brain doesn't even equate to one — it will function at a lesser capability, as will the individual as they will be experiencing conflict.

For example, organisations develop collective beliefs about the capability of their salesforce to perform, of their managers to teach and otherwise enhance the lives of their workforce, and of their administrators and policymakers to create environments conducive to these tasks. Organisations, as well as individuals, also create beliefs that are not positive — they cannot gain additional sales, clients, revenue, etc. Collectiveness creates a culture which needs to be managed.

Organisations with a strong sense of positive collective perception exercise empowering and vitalising influences over their employees. These effects are evident in their results.

The power of others' attitudes (as mentioned previously) are contagious and will affect your motivation. If you are in the company of a high sender of negative emotion, you will be affected. If you are in the company of a high sender of positivity, it will be less influential.

As the saying goes, it only takes one bad apple to spoil the barrel.

Weed out the bad apples and your motivation will improve. Take on more of the good apples that are doing the same thing that you want to do and your motivation will improve by leaps and bounds.

CHOICES

Only you can justify the choices you make and most of you will make your choices in reference to past experiences rather than future opportunities. Change how you think and you will change your future.

"The definition of insanity is doing the same thing over and over again and expecting a different result."

– Albert Einstein

How do you change to get a different result? It's easy, think differently and take different actions. Open your mind and your being to possibilities; your past does not have to equal your future. With #ConsciousLeadership it can all change.

Every thought, every action, and every decision you make takes you closer to, or further away, from where you want to be. The smallest of decisions compounded over time creates massive change. Rather than attempt to make a huge change overnight, which can be scary and overwhelming, make small incremental changes that lead you towards your goal.

What do I mean? 5 minutes exercise a day wont make much difference if you do or don't do it BUT 5 minutes everyday will. A cake on one day wont make much difference to your health BUT a cake every day will (in the wrong direction). Delaying cutting the lawn for one day wont make much difference BUT delaying every day will.

Even doing nothing takes you further away because everything else is moving forward. The skills of yesteryear will not suffice in the next year. Think about how technology changes. If you haven't kept up with the last change you will soon be a very long way behind!

Sometimes, it can be a life-changing event that allows you to make the decision to do something immediately that you have tried before and failed at. A friend of mine, when diagnosed with cancer, stopped smoking overnight after 40 years. Please do not leave it until that type of thing happens before you change. Take on board #ConsciousLeadership now and change your life for the better, it is your choice!

Start to work now on different decisions for what you want and need:

- Why wait to be taken through a disciplinary process at work before you improve your skills or performance?

- Why wait until you are so over or underweight before you change your nutrition intake?

- Why wait until you cannot walk upstairs without puffing before you increase your fitness level?

- Why wait until you are close to retirement to think about how much money you need to live on and enjoy your retirement?

Through reading, applying, and practicing the experiences of others, you can learn what has worked for those before you, and you can apply those principles in your own life.

Motivational states are directive, they guide behaviours toward satisfying specific goals or specific needs. Do you have clearly defined goals? If you don't, sit down now, identify what it is you really want or need, and write that down. Then create a plan of how you will achieve it. This will provide you with motivation to do things differently.

If you want more information on how to this, I can highly recommend my book 'The Life Changing Magic of Setting Goals'. It is available from Amazon or through ClaimYourDestiny.global

"Change begins with your awareness that your beliefs are a choice; all beliefs, conscious or unconscious, are based on a choice."

ClaimYourDestiny.global   #ConsciousLeadership

There are a myriad of choices to be made all of the time. If you choose a different way to do something, gather information that allows you to make an educated choice for action. Do your research and due diligence and pick the best solution for you.

This will enhance your confidence, create new knowledge, quieten the inner doubting voice, match your values, enhance your beliefs, or question them to bolster your attitude.

This will allow you to convince your unconscious that you are looking after it and it will help you. Provide your unconscious with the reason why you are making alternate choices to that of the past and it will support you all the way.

DELAYED GRATIFICATION

There have been many studies done related to the benefits of delayed gratification. What does this really mean? It means living with the future in mind rather than the present.

In this world of instant gratification, keeping up with the Joneses, wearing the right designer labels, being influenced by adverts that say you must have this face cream and that aftershave, feeling like your holidays must become bigger and more expensive, having to change your car every two years, etc. It can be hard to resist the instant temptation, to be outside the norm, or to exclude yourself from your friends' activities.

In the moment, sometimes it can seem obvious to take the reward, and worry about the future in the future.

Your choice is dependent on your goals, your drivers, your beliefs (and how strong they are), and how strong your will to resist temptation is.

If you can recognise when you have an opportunity for a larger or more important reward, it shows you know the difference between your needs and your wants. When you can recognise these situations, there are key terms you must think of.

Patience, will, and self-control are all characteristics of people who are masters of their environment. One common challenge is postponing immediate gratification in the pursuit of long-term goals. Delayed gratification is the process of transcending immediate temptations to achieve long-term goals.

Knowing how to create, manage, and control your goals is the first step towards completing the things you want most in life; with a goal, we engage our brain to work toward it.

Think of goals as roadmaps designed to keep you on target. They make the experience and the journey possible and more enjoyable. They, in fact, become priorities that drive our actions. They become motivators.

Let me ask you once again:

- What are your long-term goals?
  And for some of you

- What are your short-term goals?

If you do not have goals sit down now and plan them for yourself, tell yourself and others they are important, write them down and believe you are worthy of them and you will achieve them. Focus on them and they will become a reality

See
Say
Write
Believe
Achieve

ClaimYourDestiny.global

TM

THE POWER OF QUESTIONS

Questions, when constructed in the right way, are the most powerful way to access your beliefs. And this works irrespective of who asks the question. Ask yourself a question and your mind will do its best to provide you with an answer. The better your question, the better the answer.

Do you want to spend the rest of your life figuring out how to get the things you desire, or would you rather put all the guesswork behind you and get down to the fun of building an out-of-this-world lifestyle? Easy choice, right? Then do yourself a favour: suspend your disbelief, lower your shields, and try a simple way of improving your life.

Identify someone you respect who's already experiencing what you're after, find out what questions they habitually ask themselves to achieve those experiences, then use those questions yourself.

This is a globally powerful approach to success that can get you the things you want more quickly than anything else I've discovered. The habitual questions that others ask themselves when asked by yourself, to yourself can transform your life. You don't even need to understand how it all works really, although the answer's quite simple:

"When you change your habitual questions, you change your beliefs, when you change your beliefs, you change your actions, when you change your actions you change your results."

ClaimYourDestiny.global   #ConsciousLeadership

Try it! Take the time to prove to yourself that it works, that it can change the level of pain and pleasure in your life. If you like the results, keep using the questions you've discovered until they become second nature. Do this and you won't care about the why's and the wherefore's. You'll be too busy! You'll have learned firsthand there's nothing more powerful than a good question followed by action.

Ask different questions, and you will end up thinking different thoughts, saying different words, taking different actions, and getting different results. When you go one step further by modeling the questions of successful people, you're helping to ensure that the different results you're pursuing are also good results. In other words, you've done everything you can to arrive at a different place — a good place — to develop different beliefs, which are also profitable beliefs, and to become a different person who is more like the people you admire.

FOCUS

So what does all this mean really?

It means that by looking at why you do what you do and the beliefs behind that, you can basically change the thoughts and motives that direct your behaviour so that you achieve a different result, start a new job, get a promotion, create your own business, leave a relationship, start a relationship, have that difficult conversation, learn to swim, fly a plane, or simply eat a new food; the list is endless.

It is your choice completely — where your focus goes your energy flows — so change your focus to change your results.

Some of our important choices have a timeline. If you delay a decision, the opportunity is gone forever. Sometimes your doubts will stop you from making a choice that involves change and an opportunity may be missed. If you really truly want to change, start now — now is as good a time as any.

Create and ClaimYourDestiny.global through #ConsciousLeadership

My Facebook page and group is ClaimYourDestiny or you can follow me on Twitter @JulieHogbin. Visit ClaimYourDestiny.global for more articles and up to date information, plus various other social media channels and Linkedin. My hashtag is #ConsciousLeadership if you would like to find me.

> There are seven days in the week and someday isn't one of them!
>
> ClaimYourDestiny.global
> @JulieHogbin
> #ConsciousLeadership

Motives and motivation are a matter of choice — yours! Choose well, look at why you believe what you believe, and question it. Listen to the answers of the questions you ask and you will create a different future if you really want to.

My final questions to you are:

- How much do you want to change?

- How willing are you to do what is required?

- What do you need to do right now?

Good luck with whatever it is you want to do. Here's to your fabulous success; you know where to find me.

Julie xx

156

Personal Branding

"The B.R.A.N.D Process" and How to Position Yourself as an Authority Within Your Industry

MAYOORAN SENTHILMANI & LABOSSHY MAYOORAN

WHAT IS YOUR BRAND? WHY NOW?

What do you think of when you hear the name Mercedes? Or how about Starbucks? When we think about particular brands we will of course think about the logo or colours associated with their names. But what about feelings? Or desires? Or what they stand for? For example, when looking just at car companies you may associate the idea of prestige with Mercedes, the feeling of reliability with Toyota and the essence of safety with Volvo.

Successful brands have taken the time to strategically develop themselves over years and to really hone in on how they will truly set themselves apart from the competition. They have taken the steps to ensure that they stay away from the realm of brand mediocrity. Brand mediocrity occurs when a brand attempts to spread their focus too thin, and cover too many angles of the business. Of course, there is always room to ask "Well, what about this angle?" or "Maybe the consumer will appreciate this aspect." However, if one stays stuck in a constant cycle of examination without really honing in on one excellent thing about their company, then their consumers will be left with too many messages about the company being presented to them at the same time. In this scenario, it's possible that nothing will ever really "stick" in a consumer's mind. This can take the POWER away from a brand and therefore leave them in a state of mediocrity where they're lumped in with many other businesses that are aiming to provide the same product, as opposed to a business standing out from the crowd based on their own clear brand.

Staying away from brand mediocrity can really be achieved by asking yourself "Who are you?" What is the one thing that best represents you and what your consumers care about most deeply? You really need to decide on ONE THING. This can then be the one driving force you anchor to when presenting your brand to the world. All things must always lead back to this one focus. This is the one reason your brand exists. This is the one reason your business is the business that it is. All the other elements of branding will consistently point back to that one thing. From the colour of your logo to images you choose to represent a particular marketing campaign to people you may involve in promoting your product and brand. All avenues will always lead back to this one defining thing that will drive your brand to success.

Then and only then, will you truly have a powerful brand! Time and time again we have seen this in our clients. This missing piece of the branding puzzle. They are constantly trying to do too much and stretching their focus over too many avenues when trying to connect with their audience. We have worked with clients established in business who were looking for an overhaul because their brand just wasn't "working," to new businesses starting from scratch, wanting to jump into the market and really not sure of how to get started. Creating a brand is a PROCESS. This is not an overnight solution. It is about working through particular steps in order to watch your audience grow. The audience is there. Trust us! But the only way to truly harness the power of your own unique brand is working through some particular steps and honing in on what makes you special and stand out from the crowd.

With over 10 years of experience working with clients and watching them succeed, we have developed a step-by-step process to help you understand your brand and your clients' needs so that you may harness the power of your ONE THING and grow your business to great heights! Our B.R.A.N.D. Process is a simple and comprehensive way to start where you are with what you have and empower yourself to build a brand that will not only stand alone, it will stand out and shine!

Before we jump into the B.R.A.N.D. Process, we'd like to cover the basics of brand perception, what that is and how it will directly affect you. We will then move on to outlining the steps of the B.R.A.N.D. Process in a simple and comprehensive manner. We believe it does not matter if you are in at the ground level or have many years of business behind you. Our approach has the ability to take your brand to new levels of success!

BRAND PERCEPTION: WHAT IT IS AND HOW TO SHIFT IT

Do you know what people think of when they hear your brand name? Do you have a grasp on what your audience and consumers associate you with? The bottom line concept of brand perception is how your consumers see your brand. While the idea is simple, really understanding what that is for you right now may actually be more of a hurdle than you think. Your brand perception, while influenced by you, is not always easy to affect your consumers with. Sometimes you may see a "6" and they may as well see a "9." We can never fully control all the positives and negatives that will be associated with our brand. However, we want to guide you on how you can find out what the more negative perceptions may be and shift those into becoming positive ways to strengthen your brand. Your brand perception serves you and your business on the highest level, so we cannot emphasize enough the importance of really understanding and knowing what it is.

The first hurdle is to understand your current brand perception. This is the basic idea that when you simply identify what your audience currently believes about your brand, you will be able to then create a strategy to change that perception to align with how you WANT your brand to be perceived, heard and related to. Even if you think you already know, doing this work is crucial and really may surprise you at the end of the day!

This goes beyond just sales and building businesses. This is also about your brand's reputation. Think about it. Not only are people possibly engaging with you because of what you really stand for, but they may also be influenced by your pure reputation. Those are a lot of potential customers to consider!

Your reputation can influence everything from the type of consumer who will buy your product to how much they will actually pay for it to which retailers may stock it (if it is a physical product on the market). Having a positive and well-regarded reputation alone can have a massive impact on the direct success of your business. A great example is the possibility of your brand being labelled as "low quality" after a poorly managed product recall. Or perhaps you are more of what is known as a "legacy brand" that has stood the test of time, but you notice that over the years sales begin to decline as younger consumers don't see you evolving or "changing with the times," so to speak. This can be gradual and deadly!

Here's the bottom line: even if your brand image is failing, it is possible to turn things around and create a brand and business that can once again thrive. But the key is to not be afraid of really investing the time and energy into examining your brand perception. No matter what you find lurking in this unmapped territory, even if it is disheartening or more negative than you thought, we know you can turn this around for your business and brand, and continue to grow and build the client base of your dreams! You must be willing to see the darkness in the light!

Let's cover how to shift your brand perception in 5 steps. Notice how we are not saying "easy steps" as everyone's business and brand will be in different places. However, these are tangible actions you can take to understand where you are now with your brand. This is key before diving into our B.R.A.N.D. Process. Changing public opinion may seem like a difficult task to take on if you can't hire a big PR firm and invest millions into advertising, etc., but like many things in life and business, small efforts can add up to big change. Let's learn how to generate some clever in-house ideas and put them into practice.

HOW TO SHIFT BRAND PERCEPTION

1. Take inspiration from competitors

Do you know what your closest competitor is doing to effectively promote themselves? Looking at this can provide you and your team with a plethora of ideas on how you too may up the ante in the promotion department. This isn't about copying. This is about examining what is working for another brand that not only may have the same consumer base, but also may be utilizing the same resources as you when it comes to promoting your brand and product. You do yourself a disservice to try to compare yourself to and imitate a mega-brand in your field. Their resources will far outperform yours. Let's start with what you have and build from there.

An excellent first step is creating a consumer questionnaire. This is something you can create with the intention of understanding what brands are making an impact on them, which messages are resonating the most with them and how they are receiving these messages. For example, perhaps you discover that your competitor's customers just love what they share on their YouTube channel. Or perhaps their customers seem to really engage with the way the other company utilizes influencers in your field.

Another great way to gain some value is by utilizing competitor tracking tools. These can help you keep tabs on the content your rivals are producing and actually see how successful it is performing. An example of this may be discovering that your competitor is publishing very popular how-to videos that are receiving a high number of social shares. Perhaps then this may be something you want to try yourself! If you share the same consumer base, then something like this may be successful for you as well. You can even utilize these tools to target relevant influencers who may be able to spread the messages about your brand to a wider audience.

There are many tools readily available online that you can implement and use right away. Learning and understanding how your competitors are performing compared to your own brand is essential in heightening and improving your own brand perception.

2. Have an internal brainstorm (creating a new brand strategy)

Take all the data compiled from step 1 and create a comprehensive snapshot of what you have learned. Analyze the responses you have received from your questionnaire and clearly outline your strengths and weaknesses. From here you may have a few issues that you need to address.

One issue may be that you have strong in-house brand values and a well-developed brand culture, but on the outside, they are not translating or being seen by the world (the consumers). You then have to sit down and brainstorm ideas for communicating them to your audience as these are core parts of your brand.

Or perhaps after conducting some consumer research you obtain a far better idea of what truly makes your consumers tick and therefore are able to develop messages that resonate with and affect them. From here, perhaps you can brainstorm some creative concepts to test and launch on smaller scales before investing large amounts on grand scale promotions.

The flip side to this is discovering that you don't have a clearly defined brand image to start with. You then need to go back to the beginning and identify what you stand for (as touched upon earlier). This then may lead to a complete rebranding to ensure you have an identity that is recognizable and consistent throughout your operations. If this is a path you discover is necessary, don't forget that you can now utilize your tools to test aspects of your branding, such as logos and slogans, before implementing them 100 percent.

As you can see, compiling the info is one part of the solution. The other is taking all the data acquired and applying it.

3. Making it a priority

Shifting perceptions of your brand will not happen overnight. You need to make a commitment to this undertaking and realize that it won't happen by itself. It requires time, commitment and energy. After the research and brainstorming, it is then up to individuals to actually make it happen. We like the idea of creating a sort of brand perception task force to take it on. Or depending on the size of your company perhaps it is one individual that is assigned this task, and it becomes their exclusive role. It is a matter of creating direct accountability for the work to be done. Ensure that the company is making it a priority by assigning it to be someone's main focus.

If this isn't one person's sole focus, it may take them away from other projects they are currently working on. Support them in resources and time to do the job effectively. Even though you may be rerouting some work for the time being, you must keep in mind that the changes you wish to put into play will affect your long-term brand health and overall profitability. The future of your brand is worth making sacrifices for! Never forget this and ensure that everyone is on the same page. Creating strong foundations for the future is the way to make a strong and profitable brand.

4. Set S.M.A.R.T. goals

We find that our clients will succeed in this work when they create SMART goals around the action plan of improving their brand perception. This involves detailing the action plan for each initiative you've come up with during your brainstorming phase and drawing up a timeline for delivery.

Creating SMART goals when it comes to your business is an extremely effective way to make sure things get done. SMART is an acronym you can use when detailing each goal individually.

S - Specific

M - Measurable

A - Achievable

R - Relevant

T - Timely

Specific: You want to ensure the goal or action to be taken is specific. Keeping it too broad will soften the effectiveness of the product and will be hard to keep accountable.

Measurable: You want to grow your business. You want to increase your sales. (Of course!) But by what percent? When we attach actual measurable numbers to a goal, it keeps it laser focused.

Achievable: Get real with yourself and your business. It is of no use to anyone to aim TOO high. There is a fine balance between reaching beyond what you have now and trying to reach so far that you will never be able to reach your goal no matter how hard you try!

Relevant: Does it directly relate back to your major goal of improving your brand perception? Or are you focusing on something that has nothing to do with it?

Timely: Put a deadline on it. Always. Creating by-when dates in our calendar is KEY to ensuring these tasks will actually get done. It also holds people accountable for their work and creates a sense of drive towards a finish line.

A simple example of changing an idea to a SMART goal is as follows:

- **Idea**: I want better brand perception.

- **SMART goal**: I want a 20 percent increase in consumers identifying our brand as high quality by the end of the next business quarter.

Also, don't forget that setting short-term goals that fit into your long-term goal and vision will give you a higher chance of achieving it. What's more, consistently being able to track your progress is a great motivator for you and your team!

5. Measure brand perception regularly

Accessing a clear and comprehensive snapshot of your current brand's strengths, weaknesses and opportunities for growth is the last key element in shifting your brand perception. In order to know if you are meeting your goals, you will need to do this on a regular basis. This isn't a one-time thing. You want to be repeating surveys (or whatever tool you are using to measure your brand perception) on the regular so that you may have the ability to benchmark your progress.

Once you have hit your initial targets, don't stop focusing on your brand perception. The work in this aspect of your business is never done. It's a moveable feast and it can change, even if you don't. For example, trends can come and go, and you may find yourself not as relevant as you once were with your audience. However, if you are constantly keeping your finger on the pulse of how people are relating to your brand, then you will be able to move with the trends, continue to engage people and build business.

NEVER FORGET: BRAND PERCEPTION IS OWNED BY THE CONSUMER, NOT BY THE BRAND!

How can brand association play into the big picture?

Before we delve into the B.R.A.N.D. Process, it would be a disservice to you to not briefly touch upon the power of brand association.

Everything you do, say, share and feel is part of your brand. Brand associations are the mental connections between a brand and people, places, things and emotions. When a thought and a brand are connected in one's mind they neurologically connect and are more likely to be automatically associated in the future. This can easily turn people towards or away from your brand. Being mindful and even strategic about these connections will build your brand equity effectively.

Now that we have talked about the importance of having a strong brand, building brand perception and brand association, we are excited to share with you the 5 key steps involved in personal branding, The B.R.A.N.D. Process:

B - Believe

R - Relevant

A - Analyze

N - Niche

D - Define

1. BELIEVE: Believe in your brand

A brand is not just something that defines your business, a brand is born inside you. It's the thought that starts a revolution. It's the motivator that makes your vision become a reality. Believing in your brand provides consistent clarity and motivates your business and the people working for you. Most importantly, you want to create a brand that your customers can also believe in. That is the core of what you are really trying to achieve. When people believe in your brand, they trust you. When they trust you, they buy from you. But it all starts with you believing in your brand from the inside.

2. RELEVANT: The most successful brands are the most relevant brands

A quick look at some of the world's most recognized brands bolsters the notion that the most successful companies are also often the most relevant. These brands are willing to do things a bit differently. They are willing to evolve by watching what the market is doing and then by anticipating what their customers will want tomorrow.

Consumers respect brands that "get with the times" in terms of understanding what they want. They want to be reached in new and innovative ways and be consistently delivered products and services that surpass their expectations. This is what being relevant is all about.

For example, ten years ago Nokia was the leader in mobile devices but over time they failed to truly innovate and stay current. Apple was able to capitalize on this opportunity and entered the mobile device market. By offering consumers extra features and continuous innovation, Apple became the first trillion-dollar turnover company in the world in 2018. Another great example is Kodak. Ten years ago Kodak used to be the leading camera brand and but ask the younger generation now about them and they will not have a clue of what that brand represented. Nikon and Canon have overtaken the market by making photos digital and continuously innovating their products with the times. One final example is the video rental and retail chain Blockbuster, who failed yet again to innovate with the times. When Netflix came onto the scene, they created a platform for online subscription-based streaming you can watch on your own tv, which created a change for the entire film industry. They truly innovated by giving consumers the convenience they were craving.

3. ANALYZE: Analyze your brand

Brand analysis is the process of developing brand strategies, plans, evaluations, metrics and estimates for your business. It is a systematic and disciplined approach to business.

Here are some common examples of brand analysis:

- Brand Strategy: Developing or evaluating brand strategies, including elements such as brand identity and visual branding.

- Brand Architecture: Developing or evaluating structures for multiple products under a brand

- Internal Branding: Evaluating gaps between your brand promise and operational realities such as your customer service culture

- Competitive Analysis: Evaluation of your position relative to the competition. For example, developing a S.W.O.T. (Strengths, Weaknesses, Opportunities, Threats) analysis for your brand

- Market Analysis: Market analysis such as looking at the shifting demographics, values and needs of customers

- Brand Metrics: Developing brand metrics such as a brand awareness rate or top of mind

- Brand Value: Developing financial estimates for the value of a brand, typically done in the context of mergers and acquisitions

NOTE: Auditing your online presence can fall under this as well. Every tweet you send, post you share, and status update you make contributes to your personal brand. Always be mindful about creating content that is in line with your brand.

Undergoing the correct analysis of your brand will lead you to the starting point of building the authority of your brand.

BUILDING BRAND AUTHORITY AND HOW IT DRIVES GROWTH

Brand authority refers to the trust your brand has earned from customers by being seen as an expert in your field. This usually occurs because of robust and compelling content, an active online presence and social media engagement. Building brand awareness in tandem with online authority can accelerate conversions for your business. A strong brand will attract a loyal customer base that will seek you out first before turning to your competitors.

5. NICHE: Zeroing in on your niche in the market

It goes without saying that you should always strive to offer a high-quality product and great service to your clients. When trying to get ahead of your competitors though, having a niche or being the best at one particular thing will give you the competitive edge. By defining your own "micro-specialisation" (becoming an expert on a specialized topic) you will carve out a niche business.

It's all about specificity. Your niche must directly relate to a specific age group, gender or business/product.

6. DEFINE: Define your brand.

As we discussed before, improving your brand identity begins with understanding your current brand identity and improving on that. We find the best businesses follow Simon Sinek's "Golden Circle" concept: they focus on the WHY behind their business, rather than what they do or how they do it. People do not buy WHAT you do, they buy WHY you do it. If you keep this at the forefront of your plan, you will naturally engage existing and potential consumers. Simply put, your branding should resonate with your mission and vision statement (some of the very first things we touched upon at the beginning of the chapter).

This will also easily tie into telling a story through your brand and engaging people by exciting them on how you have helped others and could help them. Honing in on your "story" is a great opportunity to highlight your successes while sharing your vision with customers and employees.

We are excited to have taken you through not only the concept of personal branding but our very own 5 step B.R.A.N.D. Process. We know that if you choose to begin the journey of creating your personal brand you will add value to your business beyond your own expectations. We want you to lead a business that has passion and purpose in the market. Beyond that you should have fun while leading a determined team who wants to succeed. We know you can create this business (and life!) for yourself.

If you are ready to delve into the B.R.A.N.D Process and connect with your brand perception, and how it is affecting your business, we would love to offer you a free consultation. We want you to take your brand and your business to the next level, no matter where you are starting from!

Contact us: info@dvgstar.com

Think in Solutions – Your Way to Success

ASTRID SCHMITT-BYLANDT

How easy is it to say "this is not possible", or "I can't do this", or even worse, "you can't do this"? Then we move on and don't give the issues a second thought. I have these situations in my office every day and every time I challenge my colleagues by asking, "Imagine I wasn't here – what would you do?" Miraculously, everyone can always come up with a solution.

Don't get me wrong. That solution might not always be the one that we go with or one that works, but unless you change your thought process and your mindset, there will be many things that you are able to achieve but don't, because you are not even trying! When you feel like saying "I don't know

173

how" or "that's not possible", make a point to always come up with at least ONE solution. Start today.

Different ways of changing thought processes work for different people. Make a list, write down all solutions you can come up with, even the funny, the weird and the "impossible" ones. Even the silly ones. Discuss the issue with someone you don't know that well to get a different perspective.

One of my friends challenged me the other day and asked me, "How about we do some magic and conjure up a perfect partner, boss or staff?" Yes, I know, magic has not exactly been perfected yet. However, by brainstorming and writing down all your thoughts, you can develop your list and start working towards your solutions. Once you start this habit you will come up with a variety of suggestions that you might not have initially thought about. Step by step, you will develop new thought processes.

So many people come up with the things that are "not possible" as it is so easy to focus on the negative. Make TODAY the day you stop this habit! Let today be the start of Thinking in Solutions!

In my office, I have five key points that everyone has to learn for growth and success:

1. Assumption is the mother of all f**k-ups.

2. Take responsibility for all your actions.

3. Be persistent – always chase and follow up.

4. Always connect with new people and continue building your network.

5. Think in Solutions!

The first four could fill a whole book but I will only go through them briefly in this chapter. However, the last point is a real passion of mine. People that have taken my training and/or in my employment that understand this, progress is exponential. It is phenomenal to watch their improvement and development every single time. (For more in-depth details, please visit my website at www.solutions-finder.com, see how I can help you find your solution.)

Last year, one of my colleagues told me that a specific castle and garden in England was not allowing groups for sightseeing. I asked for the phone number and spoke to the person in charge. Let's call him Jim. We chatted for a few minutes and then I told Jim about our client who really wanted to see the castle and gardens. I told Jim that our client was coming from abroad and would there be any way this group's visit could be made possible within the set of restrictions of the castle.

I simply asked if this could be made possible. I worked around HIS and his company's needs, and I tried to find common ground. He said ok but only in the afternoons and the group could not have their own guide. They would need to go through as individuals. That was ok with the group and EVERYONE was happy. I offered to pre-pay for the entrance fees immediately and when it came to booking again this year, Jim was happy to take another two groups the same way. Despite initially being told it was not possible, I was able to work out a deal that worked for everyone.

Think: What can I do for you? What would work for you? How can I help you?

A few years ago, I helped one of my friends who produces high quality rain and greywater harvesting solutions for airports, housing and other big building projects, to get an appointment with a specific engineer, who seemed to be blocking my friend's systems for all of his construction projects. My friend found it impossible to get hold of this particular engineer. Again, I asked for the phone number, I picked up the phone, asked for the engineer, got him on the phone, and arranged a time for a meeting with my friend. Now you might think, everyone can get lucky. Of course! However, this barrier my friend had in his head regarding the engineer being hard to get hold of didn't exist for me. I picked up the phone as if to call my mum or my friends. In my mind, there was no issue. I had no negative thoughts on this. In fact, I had no thoughts other than wanting to schedule a meeting. Had the engineer not been in the office, I would have asked his colleague for a time to call back. If the engineer had still not picked up, I would have asked to have a meeting or phone conversation scheduled. If you really want something, then persistence is one way to bring solutions.

Think: Be results driven and never give up!

For me, the word 'no' from someone else just doesn't resonate unless I have tried myself. Of course, it's not always possible to get someone to say 'yes'. You might say, "I can't go over my boss's head" or "I can't constantly do other people's work if they don't achieve what they should". No, I am not saying you should. You also have to cut your losses and think about what your time is worth to YOU. Perhaps your time is spent better achieving something else. Are there other ways or other things that you should be doing instead? Just because I can spend a lot of time on achieving something that others tell me is not possible doesn't mean I should necessarily do it.

However, it is crucial that, in order to start thinking in solutions, you change your thought process. Ask yourself if anyone famous you can think of could achieve what you want to achieve and might get a 'yes' in a situation that you feel is 'impossible'. If the answer is "yes," then your focus needs to be:

- How do you think they would do it?

- How can I or we make it possible?

- What does it need?

- Who could I ask for help?

- What solutions can I or we think of?

Money, I hear you say, is what makes most things happen. And yes, you are right. If you have a lot of money, you can employ more people. It's easier to ask people for favors and you might have a bigger network of people with skills, talents and contacts. Yes, money makes it easier, but that doesn't mean that things are otherwise impossible!

Solutions come in a variety of forms. Brainstorming is just one way. Always keep in mind: different people equal different views. Talk to your work team as well as the few key people that are part of your inner circle. Speak to the people from your sports groups or any of the groups that you might belong to. Ignore your habit of thinking that the issue might be difficult or impossible. Start fresh, every time! If your mind is focused on solutions, creating new ways and thinking about new routes and methods will become second nature. You'll surprise yourself with what you can actually achieve in life, in love and in work.

Think: If you need new inspiration, change your surroundings.

Change the people that you speak to about your issues. Change the environment you are sitting in or working in, or even where and how you sit. Change your lunch or dinner routines. Change your route to work or your gym routine. Give yourself a chance to gain different perspectives. Start meeting new people. Start networking with different people from different professional and social circles. Start new evening courses, read new books, find new things to do in your spare time. Nothing should keep you from finding the solutions that will lead you towards your path of success.

START WITH YOUR ROUTINES AND YOUR LANGUAGE

Often, we don't even notice when something has become a routine or a habit. Our minds do it on autopilot. We may get to our destination without having a conscious memory of the events that got us there. Even when there's a shift in our routine, it can be hard to break habits and we might find ourselves continuing to follow the same path because it's convenient or easier.

A few weeks ago, my normal route to work was blocked. I had to take a detour. Even on day two, three and four, I forgot that my "normal" route was closed. For days, I drove around the corner of my house right into the "road ahead closed" sign. I am sure we have all been in that situation before. We do something every day and it becomes a this-is-how-it's-meant-to-be way.

Actively find other ways and always know that you have the power to act.

Your daily routines often dictate your reality. Stop for a moment and think about what you did yesterday. Make one small change TODAY.

I can already hear the excuses about why it is not possible to change your life:

- But I can't…

- But how?

- But my kids, husband, family, boss, friends, etc.

- But I don't know…

- But I don't have the money…

- But I don't have time…

STOP!

Start with the mindset of searching for your solutions. Finish with the mindset that is focused on the obstacles. Time and money are something we can all make if it is important enough!

Think: Stop your routines – replace them with new ways.

DAILY LIFE SCENARIOS THAT CRY OUT FOR NEW SOLUTIONS

These are a few typical scenarios I see in my coaching sessions. Within a short chapter I can, of course, only scratch the surface of how things can be worked on and tackled. But here are a few examples:

Relationships

If your relationship is on the brink of failure, start by asking yourself:

1. What does my partner want from this relationship? (yes, start with your partner and not with yourself!)

2. What do I want from this relationship?

3. How can we successfully move forward setting goals and breaking them down into small steps?

4. What is the measurement to know when I have achieved step one?

5. What can I do to take the next step?

Then set steps two, three and four - one at a time.

Implement each small step immediately and start the change now! Remember, though, it might well be that what the other side wants is just not what you want. Sometimes, it is time to move on. However, without starting to find common solutions, you will continue in the same rut, day in, day out.

Moving house

You want a new house? Then go out and find it! Define what it is that you want, where you want to live, how you want to live - SEE where and how you want to live! Visualize! Paint a picture or cut out the kind of housing that you can see yourself living in from ads or magazines. Go to the areas you want to live in, check the schools, the bars, the sports clubs or whatever it is you are looking for. Analyze your situation and determine what your options are. Do you have enough money for a deposit? Can you re-mortgage your current home? Can you sell your home and then move? Can you borrow money? Can you make extra money by taking in a lodger for a period of time to build up your savings? Can you move to a different area which is cheaper or closer to work or your children's school? Can you save money by doing or not doing things? Can you rent out a room to a language school and take in a student for a few months each year? Can you rent out a room on Airbnb? Tackle the "what" and "where" first and then tackle the financial side exactly the same way. But again, you need to start and take action NOW.

I won't go into the financial side as many books have been published about this and one paragraph will not do it justice. However, I would like to mention this sudden realization from one of my staff. I'll call her Rita:

Rita: "I just bought my lunch. I bought one of the plastic bags to carry the stuff back to the office. The bag costs GBP 0.10, which is not that much. But, if I went shopping three times a week and had started shopping at 10 years old, by the time I turned 90 I would have spent GBP1,248 in plastic shopping bags!!! That's two holidays for me!!"

New job needed

Unhappy with your job? Then find a new one! Easier said than done, some of you will say. Whatever the reasons you might have for not changing there is a solution! Focus on the positive even if you have been unemployed! What skills do you have? What makes you happy all day, every day? What do you really want to work in? What new qualifications might you need? How can you get them? Who can you ask to help you prepare your CV or prepare you for interviews? Who can you ask who might know someone in the field you would like to go into? What do you love doing? Who does what you do or want to do? Find that person who is successful at what you would like to do! See if you can work with or for them. If necessary, offer to work for free for a week or more to show that you are the right person for the job. If that is not possible, try and work on a few weekends or in the evenings. Find five or ten potential ways and explore all of them to find your perfect solution. Adjust your outcomes each time to move in the right direction.

Decide:

1. What is it that I actually want?

2. What and how does that look like and feel like?

3. What do I believe is holding me back?

4. How can I solve the issues that I believe are holding me back?

5. What is the timeframe I want this change to happen in?

6. Who can I ask for help?

Start researching your new job options. Start scheduling those interviews. Plan for what you are looking for. Are you a part-time mum interested in a part-time job? Or, do you want a bit more income as a pensioner or perhaps the multi-million-pound new job! Focus on what you want and work on finding the right solution every day.

Every new step has to be planned and you have to start TODAY! Just like learning how to walk, take a baby step each day. Only you can take these steps. No one will do it for you.

Actively change your ways. Get those different perspectives. Shake up your routine by trying something new or different. You can't reap the benefits of change without shifting your mindset and perceptions. You have to find the right solutions for yourself.

Think: Action, even in the form of a small step, is a step in the right direction!

THE ADVANTAGE OF COACHING

Remember when your parents, siblings or teachers said, "Do you want to learn how to walk, talk? Play the piano? Play tennis, football, etc.?" Each day you improved a little bit by following a step by step process. Today, you can swim, play tennis, speak a language, or whatever you started learning in your earlier years.

If, today, you had someone who said, "I know how to do what you want to achieve. I'll take you by the hand and walk with you, come what may," wouldn't you immediately say, "YES. Please show me!"

FIND that person who has done what you want to do.

FIND that person who will listen to what you want to achieve, who can teach you what you would like to learn and hold you responsible when you slack. Be proactive and persistent in looking for the solutions that are right for YOU.

Think and write down: What do I want to achieve and what are all the ways I can think of to start me on my journey to success?

Unfortunately, as children, we don't always appreciate free education. However, as an adult, education can be expensive. All too often, we wish we had learnt languages, math, etc. at school, studied harder or been taught X-Y-Z subject, for example, business, media, making/managing money, setting up your own business, etc. There is no back to the future time machine yet but you can move forward! It is never too late to start afresh with anything you would like to have and enjoy!

My mum found love after my dad died when she was 74. She turned 92 this August and what an amazing 18 years they have already shared and hopefully, they will have many more years to come of travelling, going out and appreciating each other's company. Remember, it is never too late!

If you are ready to learn, then you can find online courses, free YouTube tutorials, sports classes, evening classes and, of course, mentors and coaches. I have helped many people through their life's crises over the years. It took a long time to fully realize that this is a skill that I hugely enjoy. I have supported many people move forward in life and achieve their goals. Now I finally made this into my perfect job. I started looking at patterns in what I was doing, and

I started thinking about how to use this to help not just my friends and my family. Since the beginning of the year I started training unemployed people to be able to go back to work. It is one of the most rewarding things I have done in my life (only beaten by having children on my own through IVF – but that's a different story).

Everyone can find a course or a trainer, a mentor or a coach. See if they have achieved what you want to achieve and work with them to set your targets and your steps. Hopefully, they can hold you accountable every step of the way and help you remain focused and disciplined, which will, therefore, achieve your desired outcome and successes.

No matter what it is that you want, there is a solution! It might require you to think outside the box, but once you do, then the possibilities are endless. How do you get the type of mindset that will have you focused on solutions?

It starts by retraining your brain to look for the positive. See challenges and address them, instead of seeing obstacles that are blocking your path to success. Accept that it can be difficult to shift your mindset after years of experiences that shaped your way of looking at your world. Give yourself some credit for starting small and being persistent! (And if you have children start them as early as possible on their "yes I can do this" way through life!)

Now, you might not realize this but language also plays a huge part in your daily achievements and your thought processes. You might not immediately think about how words and language can have a massive influence, so I would like to set a challenge for you:

For seven days, stop for a few seconds every time you THINK or SAY something negative!

If you want to keep track, open a document on your mobile phone and write down how many times a day you say something negative about work, friends, your colleagues or about your health, partner, family members or whatever you think or talk about. You'll be amazed, if you are honest with yourself, by just how many times every day you think negatively and don't even realize it. Both mentally and verbally we need to make ourselves aware every hour of the day how we think and what consequences this has on our behavior, perception and actions.

Here's a challenge for the second week: stop yourself before you say something negative and consider putting it into a positive phrase.

Instead of shouting for the tenth time at your child for not having done something you asked, take a deep breath and explain the issue. Rather than scolding or punishment, which so far has never really given you the result you have wanted, find a solution to move forward.

Instead of slagging off your colleague, just say nothing or try and actually compliment him or her. Find that one positive thing that you see in him or her.

If you know that your partner "always" forgets something, is always late, or whatever he or she might do, anticipate it. Offer your help if you are better at it and find a solution together so you can both relax.

Changing both your thought processes and your language is key to any change.

Of course, some things are harder to get done on your own. That's why working with someone who can shake up your routines, who can remind you of your goals and achievements and who can re-focus you, can be a huge source of motivation. I love my job. I love helping people who are feeling stuck in a difficult situation in their lives, shifting their mindset and helping them to set and achieve their goals. Find that person that can be your 'go to Person' to move forward.

REALIZE THE IMPACT OF YOUR HABITS, PRIORITIES AND BELIEFS

One of the realities of creating any change in your life involves recognizing how your routines, and also your habits, impact your life. That can often be harder than you realize, but once you start the process of being honest with yourself and shifting your thinking, then the impact of your habits, your priorities and your beliefs will become apparent.

One of my clients who is unemployed talked about his goal of writing his own book and opening his own small business. Throughout the process, he has taken in so much and has already moved miles forward. I am thrilled with his progress, but when we started talking about making healthy food choices, the excuses started to fly.

"I'm not good at that, it costs so much" or "What is healthy anyway?"

Every response was an excuse about why changing his eating habits was not possible. So, to help him shift his thinking, I started with something that I knew he could do, regardless of budget or time.

"Well, you can start with drinking eight free glasses of tap water every day," I said.

"Eight?"

He looked at me for a minute as if I had asked him to do something extraordinary. I confirmed that I had said eight. "Ah, I can't do this," he said.

"Why? It is free and it is so simple."

Then I shifted the topic to his dog. His eyes lit up and he spoke with such love and gratitude for his dog. "He is the one keeping me sane through my dark times, but he is old now and has hip problems," he said.

"Do you walk him every day?" I asked.

"Of course!"

"Do you feed him every day?"

"Of course!"

"And when he is thirsty, do you give him water?"

"Of course!"

"So, you look after your dog, but not yourself?"

After a long silence, he said, "Oh, I see."

Sometimes, we know what we need to do, but we don't really realize it. Or rather, we know what to do, but we choose not to act. Take the issues in your life and imagine that someone else told you about those same problems in their life. What would you say to them? What solutions would you present to them?

Write down the options that you would suggest to someone else. Then write down all your thoughts regarding the situation. Include a list of all the objections that you might have. For each objection, I challenge you to come up with one positive answer. You need to be actively searching for solutions. It is about training yourself to think in a new way, one that allows you to tap into your creative mind and the solutions that are locked up inside your mind.

The reality is that you most likely have the answers, but you are blocking them with whatever excuse you have been telling yourself. I want you to change your habits to break through those blockades. But right now, that might feel a bit overwhelming.

So, by taking small steps, you can take action daily to implement just one of the positive solutions you found. Work on them until that solution becomes one of your new habits. You will know it has truly become a habit when you don't think about it anymore, just like when you are driving a car. Then move on to the next point.

Changing a habit starts with:

- defining your goal

- finding out what your false beliefs are that hinder you and hold you back

- breaking your goal down into smaller steps

- creating a timeframe for achieving each of those smaller steps

- finding motivation by defining the "WHY"

- moving forward by completing the smaller steps

It is possible to stop habits from one day to the other, like it is possible to stop smoking, but it needs a lot more discipline and effort than many of us are willing to invest. So set for yourself small steps and small goals!

You need to actively replace every small step you set for yourself and stay focused on the solutions you have set out and defined for yourself. Each habit you replace will allow you to then shift to another one. Creating any change in your life, small or major, begins with these small changes.

Always seek positive reinforcement as that is the key to inspiring continued action. If you are trying to change everything at once, the process becomes overwhelming, and our tendency is to just give up. I want you to manage the process of change. I want the process and the small successes to motivate you and keep you moving forward.

BE CREATIVE – LOOK FOR OPPORTUNITIES EVEN WHERE YOU WOULDN'T EXPECT THEM

This tool is priceless, from working with your children or your family to working in your job, with your team, or on your relationship.

Last week, I had to take my car to a car wash. I had to do it with my 2-year-old twins, which most parents will agree is not as easy as when you do it on your own. I had to keep my children occupied for 30 minutes so we went for a walk. Now, not many 2-year-olds are hugely keen on going for a walk. They don't see that exercise is good for everyone.

As we walked through the streets, I found an empty beer can and for the next 30 minutes, we kicked the beer can through the streets back towards the garage where the shiny clean car was waiting for us. Time had flown by, even for me, and neither the picture of an empty beer can in the street nor the vision of a walk for 30 minutes while waiting for the car to be cleaned would have thrilled anyone. This walk was different! An empty beer can made it fun.

I know, you can't kick a beer can around the office, you can't kick it around at home – but you CAN take nearly any task and break it down in chunky sizes and there will always be some kind of positive angle to it. Even if it only means you got it done and can cross it off your to do list! Feel the feeling of achievement!

Think: What will make my work easier or even fun?

Are there areas in your life where you might be missing out because you are stuck seeing your world from a perspective that no longer serves you? I want you to stop looking at a situation from the same point of view and find other ways of tackling and thinking about this issue or situation. If you have discussed it with other people, and you are not getting any further, be creative! Imagine you were a famous person. How would he or she go about it? Or if you are less into this kind of creative thinking and more logical, then be creative on paper. Write a SWOT analysis (strengths, weaknesses, opportunities, threats) or just put a pros and cons list together.

START TODAY and your reality will start to shift! You will truly amaze yourself at the possibilities and opportunities that will come your way!

Even if your circumstances do not change right away, changing how you view those circumstances will allow for a change in attitude, which will lead to change in your life.

Every point in this chapter has focused on you finding solutions by opening your mind and shifting your perception. Now I want to question whether you are actually being honest with yourself and taking responsibility for your life choices or if you are essentially hiding with your head in the sand.

TAKING RESPONSIBILITY STARTS WITH HONESTY

How good are you at taking responsibility for your own actions? Be honest with yourself!

Today's culture focuses on blaming others and using circumstances outside of our control as the reason why we react or behave a certain way. It's easier to feel like a victim than to take responsibility for our own actions.

Not long after I had joined a new company, which required me to move from Germany to London, my former boss told me that it was my fault that one of the hotel contractors had missed the assigned deadline. That contractor had received the deadline from me two months earlier. Her inactions meant we lost a huge piece of business. I was livid! I had gone out and gained the client's trust, asking my boss that the company spend money on a sales trip. I had done my sales job, and now I got the blame for losing the business?! The contractor hadn't even looked at the file for the whole past two months. I was at fault? Not her?

It was a learning experience for me, one that I took with me, eventually to open my own first business. First, though, I immediately changed my way of working. Every request was put into a separate file. I started keeping count of the work that I had passed to the contributing departments. I started to chase everything! I was determined that this was never going to happen to me again.

Think: Always take responsibility!

Today as a business owner, I can better understand my former boss's point of view. It was a big piece of business, one that needed to be managed and monitored throughout the process and that should have been my job and, of course, it was in my interest to check for updates. However, I also learnt that if a member of staff can be allowed to sit on a piece of business with no one checking on the progress, then process and management also need to be checked and changed. The internal systems of each business, of course, also need to be thoroughly reviewed and analyzed.

Today, therefore, the first person I always hold accountable is myself. The responsibility for the success or failure of my businesses always lies first and foremost with me. When you are trying to make a significant change in your life or career, it can be difficult to be honest with yourself and acknowledge how you may have contributed to an outcome you didn't desire. Without that acknowledgment and honesty, however, you cannot learn and grow from your experiences.

You might not always like what you find, but if you are not honest with yourself, then you can't make changes, create a different outcome or move forward.

Think: What can I do to move things forward and what is my responsibility?

If you truly want change in your life, analyze each section and ask yourself honestly what your current status quo is.

What are you willing to accept from yourself? Where do you want to go and WHO do you want to be or become? Whether it be in family life, as a parent, as a boss, as a colleague, in your sports achievement or as a partner. Create your vision!

Push yourself out of your comfort zone! Yes, it might sometimes be uncomfortable!

It definitely was uncomfortable to hear what my boss had to say, but it allowed me to rethink my way of working, my way of thinking and to do what was necessary to change and improve the situation, both then and in my future. Mistakes are there to be made but make them just once!

Here are a few questions to help you start shifting your thinking into solution-based thinking and help you identify the ways that you might be falling into the "blame game":

• What do or did I contribute to my current circumstances, both personally and professionally?

• Have I been open to taking risks and stepping outside of my comfort zone?

- Where am I blaming others, or circumstances, rather than taking responsibility to move forward?

- Are the things that are holding me back in the past and therefore cannot be changed?

- How can I accept the past and learn to move forward?

- What small step can I set today to move me on the road for change and success?

Are you willing to break out of your comfort zone? Are you willing to really be honest with yourself? Only you are in charge of your life and it is important to take responsibility for it!

WHAT IS THE BLAME GAME?

I want to stop for a minute and talk about the blame game. Simply put, it is when you are dealing with various situations in your life and choose to blame others for your situation. You believe you are the victim, instead of focusing on what you could do to change the situation NOW. You are essentially giving away your power and allowing others to control your life. The thought process turns into one that makes everything appear impossible and out of your control, so you sit, stuck, doing nothing at all to create change in your life.

I see some of this in my clients that are unemployed. The system especially twenty or more years ago wasn't set up to identify ADHD or dyslexia or other forms of learning disabilities. Parents might have not been able to help financially or mentally and once someone is at the bottom it really is hard to get up again. Not to mention, many companies do not even give people a chance to prove themselves.

However, this absolutely does not mean you should give up! The past is the past and can never be changed. Now is the time to take responsibility, move forward, make changes, listen, learn, forgive and make that leap! Be responsible, be on time, be reliable and be flexible! All these actions anyone can do, regardless of your situation.

Here are some questions to ask yourself as you deal with various situations in your life:

- Do you blame someone for something in your life?

- Do you blame a situation for something that went wrong in your life?

- Do you appear to take responsibility, but then turn around and immediately start focusing on the actions of others?

- Do you compare your choices and actions with others, judging them as better or worse?

- Are you letting others rule your life?

- Are you not taking action because you believe nothing can be done?

Think: Let the past lie, accept what cannot be changed and take action to have that better future you deserve!

CREATING ACTIONS

No matter what circumstances we all are presented with in life, we still have the ability to act. You still control your thoughts and feelings. No one else has that control, nor should they! Even in old age you can take action, so age is no excuse! Do not become so focused on finding excuses that you block yourself from opening doors and creating opportunities for yourself.

A few weeks ago, as I sat to have a relaxing manicure, the TV screen on the wall showed a Ninja UK program where amazing young men and women go over very intense courses, challenging their own fitness, agility and power. One candidate even had only one leg.

A very big lady sitting next to me said, "Oh, I want him to win. How amazing is he!"

When coming across one exercise, which was already hugely difficult for the candidates with two legs, he failed and fell into the pool below.

The lady turned around to her waiting husband and said, "Wow, that makes me want to go to the gym."

Not in a million years did I think that she would go home and start working out. You WISH you were as fit, but you are unwilling to put in the hard work. Instead, we spend our energy coming up with excuses for why things can't get done. The reality is that you are making up reasons why you won't do it.

Think: What excuses are you using to justify why you aren't taking action?

There are so many excuses that we create to justify why we refuse to act and create change in our lives. Why do we wish for things but then take no action?

- Because it seems too hard.
- Because it seems too tiring.
- Because there does not seem to be enough time.

- Because, because, because.....

The list is long. However, there is so much that is possible when you only open up your mind and heart!

Think: The possibilities in my life are endless if I only embrace them!

Inaction, a lack of honesty with yourself and not taking responsibility are just a few of the key reasons why you might be struggling to create change in your life. By acknowledging how these reasons contribute to your current situation, you begin to change. Once you decide to change your thinking and perception, then you need to find others who support you in these efforts.

NETWORKING: BUILDING SUPPORT FOR CHANGE

One of the things so many people are afraid of seems to be networking. What is it about going to an event and talking to strangers that people worry about? Everyone is there for the same reasons. What is the worst that can happen?

You can expand your network and increase the resources available to you professionally and personally. New networks are also great ways to find individuals who can help hold you accountable or even offer you different choices for work or life. Also remember, these people also know others who might be able to help with your challenges and efforts or, of course, you can help them!

I constantly encourage people to look at who they are surrounding themselves with. Be honest with yourself about the type of thinking they represent.

Think: Is it the type of thinking you want to make a part of

your life? Do THEY lead the life you want for yourself?

Leave "friends" behind that shoot people down. They are no friends if they don't support you. They only keep you around to make themselves feel better by belittling you. Move on, there are new people to be met who will believe in what you want to achieve, and who live and breathe the solutions you need.

The people you surround yourself with can also serve as inspiration. They can get you motivated to keep tackling various challenges in your life, instead of giving up. Feelings of frustration can become blockades in your efforts to be solution oriented in your thinking.

Our inner circle, those people who support us, can be the way that you break through frustration, barriers and problems. They might even provide a few solutions you never thought of.

The more you surround yourself with solution-focused individuals, the more you will think in solutions. The same is true when you are trying to change habits or create new ones. Let's talk about how to shift them without being overwhelmed in the process.

Building a network involves finding places with like-minded individuals, be it personally or professionally. If you are looking to build a professional network, then start with industry events where you can meet other professionals who can point you to various opportunities.

Personal networking often starts with self-empowerment and growth opportunities. It could be mastermind classes or attending talks specifically focused on areas that you are trying to grow in. The point of any class or talk is about not only learning, but meeting others. You make connections that help you grow, but you might also prove to be a connection that allows them to grow.

Why should you build a network?

Here are a few of the key reasons:

- to help you explore new solutions to your challenges

- to help you meet others with different perspectives

- to challenge yourself to stretch your abilities

- for support in making shifts, personally or professionally

- to find the people to help you grow and become successful in what you want to do

- to give advice and support to others who may be in a situation similar to one you are or were in

Networking opportunities are available in a variety of areas. You can opt to search online for networking opportunities, such as those for local business owners. If you are looking for opportunities to create change in the community, then look for community get-togethers where you can meet others and build support. Or find a local charity, a new sport you can take up – the opportunities are endless.

The point is that finding networking opportunities often starts by just opening your mind and having the willingness to extend yourself beyond your current status quo. I always encourage people to build or extend their network, because doing so will give more opportunities to grow and learn. You might be thinking, "I don't have time to network. My schedule is already so full."

I understand what it means to be a busy professional. Being a single mother to my truly amazing twins and running my businesses, as well as all of my other professional endeavors, means that my schedule often seems to be running me. To make time for new networking opportunities every now and then, I have focused on prioritizing, systemizing, working hard and, where possible, delegating. It helps me to manage all my obligations and to make time for everything in my life that I find valuable, both personally and professionally. And if you still find it daunting to go networking, then come on our networking course or search for one in your area.

FINDING MOTIVATION IN YOUR LIFE

We all need motivation. I think of it as the key necessary to get the car started. Without it, you are not going anywhere. You don't start you go nowhere! However, once you start every small success will feed more success and in return will fuel your motivation.

The idea is to keep yourself motivated through the progress you make. Another way to remain motivated is of course through mentors or coaches.

Once I stared looking for and working with my mentors I truly got inspired and motivated to tackle the challenges in my life and find my solutions. Mentors keep you on your toes, and for me they continue to show me new ways of thinking that inspire me to learn and grow; every day!

Not only is it important to work with mentors, you also learn when you teach yourself. Mentoring others gives you a chance to reinforce, in your own mind, the ways that you want to think and act.

Taking action involves work, but once you get started, you will be amazed at how much better you feel. Your world will start to change because you have changed your way of thinking.

Do not be afraid to take the first steps to create change by shifting your thinking and perceptions. Once you make that shift, then you are going to find it easier to build a network, change your habits and start on the path of growth and finding solutions. My professional life benefited when I stopped making excuses or finding others to blame. The lessons I learned carried into my businesses and my personal life have assisted me in every goal that I have achieved so far.

No matter where you are in terms of your personal or professional life, do not assume that it is too late to take risks or that you cannot change. You have the power of YES to create the life that you want. It starts by changing your thinking, from searching for problems to being solution oriented.

Connect with Astrid and her team at www.solutions-finder.com and share your journey with them to find the solutions for your challenges. On the website you can share stories, learn about Astrid's events, and become the more successful YOU!

Unlocking the Secret to Success

Discovering the Power of Emotional Intelligence

RAV BAINS

WHAT IS EMOTIONAL INTELLIGENCE?

What is an emotion?

An emotion is a feeling we get as a result of something that has triggered us. This trigger can be internal or external; in other words, something that we think, see, hear, speak or do. For example, you might see two people arguing, and that could arouse some emotion in you. An example of an internal trigger could be that you think of something in the past that was negative, and this has brought up an emotion in you. The other important factor to remember is that an emotion can be strong or weak. The strength of the emotion will depend on your interpretation of what you've thought, seen, heard, spoke or done. Since we all have different values and belief systems, the event, whether internal or external, is "neutral." Why is this important to understand? Because you have a choice as to how to react to the thing that has happened! Now you might ask how this is possible. If I see a car accident how can that be neutral? Isn't it bound to evoke an emotion? Well, what is the likelihood that ten people who witnessed the accident will have the same reaction? They won't. Their reactions could range from very strong to slight, to no reaction at all. So, it's not the event, but rather your interpretation of that event that will determine the emotion. One of the reasons you blame the event for your emotional reaction is that it all happens in a fraction of a second! As a result, you confuse the trigger (the event) with your emotional reaction, which is actually determined by you. This topic always becomes an interesting conversational point in my seminars, which is great because it allows for rich understanding of emotions and triggers. The important thing to remember is that life has no meaning until we give it meaning.

What triggers an emotion?

Now that we have touched on emotions and triggers, the next critical question for you to ask is what triggers your emotions. Understanding this question is fundamental to understanding your personal and professional success or failure. You see, people never stop to think why they have an emotional reaction to something. In fact, did you know that 90% of the population don't think? (Earl Nightingale) Just because they have thoughts (which are often haphazard), they believe they are thinking. Thinking is the deliberate, conscious awareness of the thoughts you are having, and deciding what thoughts you actually want to have. The other fundamental mistake people make is that they think they are their thoughts. We aren't our thoughts. We are aware of our thoughts, so we can't be the thoughts. Now at this point you might feel a little confused.

That's ok, it will become clearer as you read on. It's critical that you get to know what triggers you. It could be what people say or do, or certain circumstances, situations or events. It's also important to be aware of the type of emotion or feeling you're getting in those situations and circumstances. These emotions will determine how you act and react. Are they positive or negative? Are they pleasurable or painful? These questions will help to determine whether you're making good judgments or not. They will also determine whether you're responding or reacting to the person, situation or circumstances. One of the other fundamental factors to remember is that human beings can trigger an emotional reaction simply by thinking bad thoughts—without anyone else interfering. So, you can get into a bad mood all by yourself!

Emotions drive behavior

Many people seem to think that their circumstances cause them to react to things, and

that's why they have an emotional reaction. As a result, they constantly blame what's happening around them, which is external to them. In my coaching sessions I've heard so many individuals complain about their partner, the kids, the boss or their team at work. It's as if they think that changing what's around them will allow them to be happy or in a better mood. This means no more emotional reaction. Well, if you've been following the earlier reading, then you'll have remembered that all events are neutral, and only you are in control of your feelings and emotions. Therefore, the mood you're in or the emotional reaction you're having to a situation or event will determine how you behave! For example, if you're in a bad mood, what's the likelihood you're going to be at your best at home or in the workplace? We can safely assume you're not going to be! What many people fail to realize is that emotions, not circumstances, drive behavior. So, how you're feeling or what kind of emotional state you're in will determine your performance and your leadership. This means that if you want to change your own or someone else's behavior you must get to the root cause of the emotion that's driving them or you, otherwise you'll be focusing your energies on the symptoms instead of causes and, as a result, be less effective in your efforts. This is one of the key elements to understand as part of EI.

Definition of EI

Now that we've established what emotions are, what triggers emotions and that emotions drive behavior, we can conclude that *EI is one's ability to understand one's emotions—what triggers them, what circumstances cause the trigger and how to regulate the emotions.* By doing this there is a good chance that you'll make better, more thoughtful decisions and have a positive impact on those around you. This means better performance by you, and the role modeling of good personal leadership.

WHAT IS WISDOM?

Wisdom is having the knowledge of what is right or true, coupled with just judgment regarding an action to be taken. The most famous example of this is the story of two women who came to King Solomon, each claiming to be the mother of a certain infant. Knowing that only one could be the true mother,

King Solomon decreed that the baby be cut in half and one part given to each woman. The true mother, unwilling to have her baby hurt in any way, revoked her claim. Solomon knew this would happen and, thus, awarded the child to that woman.

Intelligence versus Wisdom

King Solomon had to understand intelligence in order to make the decision he did ... He had to be prepared to go through with his decree. And he also had to know how the true mother would react. So, on the surface, it would seem that both intelligence and emotional intelligence are necessary for wisdom. However, if we accept that the two women were intelligent in their own way, it quickly becomes apparent that intelligence is not necessary for wisdom.

Why is this important?

Thinking is the deliberate, conscious awareness of the thoughts you're having and then deciding what thoughts you want to have. This is the exact opposite of what most people do. Most people base their actions on how they feel in the moment. They don't take time to rationalize the situation and choose an appropriate thought.

WHY DO ORGANIZATIONS NEED EMOTIONAL INTELLIGENCE?

Because there are:

- **Challenges in individual behavior** ... Once Emotional Intelligence is understood by individuals in organizations, their behavior changes dramatically. They stop reacting and start to respond thoughtfully to situations.

- **Challenges in building relationships** … If employees are unable to cooperate with each other, this will affect organizational performance. Once people start to grasp the concept and competences of self-awareness, cooperation and harmony, it will lead to better results.

- **Challenges in teamwork** … Teamwork is critical for success; however, too often individuals in teams fall into the "right wrong trap!" and individuals quickly start to take positions. Once people understand that it's all emotional, they start to focus on outcomes and results.

- **Challenges in managing change** … Organizations struggle in implementing change, and employees often resist. Fear is a big factor in change management, as people focus on what they will lose as opposed to what they will gain. People start to 'awfulize,' but once they understand that it's the relationship between the emotional mind and the thinking mind that is driving the fear, resistance disappears.

- **Challenges in achieving organizational goals** … Employees often struggle with their values versus the organization's values. They often forget what their Personal Leadership Responsibility is in the organization. Understanding the philosophy of Emotional Intelligence and personal accountability puts them back on the right track.

- **Challenges in understanding 'soft skills!'** … Organizations spend millions of dollars on driving hard for goals and results, but remain weak on developing the soft skills required by individuals and teams. They fail to realize that it's the 'soft stuff' that makes the 'hard stuff' easier! Once individuals and teams grasp this concept, they excel in all areas of their lives and get engaged actively in achieving organizational results.

The main thing to remember about Emotional Intelligence is that it can be taught, improved and used within your company to create a healthy workplace, motivate employees and achieve your goals. It's definitely a strong tool that can put you out in front of your competition. So, get from being a good organization to a great organization!

UNDERSTANDING EMOTIONS AS VIBRATIONS

One of the failures of our learning is that no one has explained to us that emotions are actual vibrations in the body. When we are angry, we don't say "I have a negative vibration" we say "I am angry!" In other words, we have made the emotion part of who we are and, as a result, we do not pay attention to the vibration. We don't realize that it's a vibration, and that we aren't our vibrations. We are aware of our vibrations. I know this might be a little confusing, BUT this is one of the keys to really grasping what is happening to us emotionally. As a result, we'll have a chance to manage our emotions and hence our behavior.

It's critical to be in tune with what is happening in the body, and paying attention when there is a change in this vibration, because then you'll know you're having a reaction to something. I can't stress enough the importance of this fact. Start paying attention to the sensations/vibrations in your body. Stop living from the neck upwards, just in the mind!

I believe you aren't going to get this important piece of information from any other emotional intelligence book or trainer.

THINK ABOUT WHAT YOU'RE THINKING

We very rarely pay any attention to our thoughts. The average person doesn't understand the importance of thinking. People assume this is an activity that just happens and that they really don't have any control over it. Wrong! If you want to change your life, then start paying attention to what you're constantly thinking about. Are your thoughts negative or positive? Why is this important? Well, thoughts arouse emotions. Earl Nightingale, in 1960, said that "90% of people simply don't think!" You see, you need to understand that activity in the mind isn't thinking. We're constantly thinking about shopping lists, work, picking the kids up, cooking, and on and on we go! Not that this isn't important, but you need to understand that you're not your thoughts. You are, however, aware of your thoughts and therefore can choose what you think about. Negative thoughts will trigger negative emotions. Conversely, positive thoughts will trigger positive emotions, which in turn puts us in a better state of mind. We as humans have so habituated negative thinking that we have normalized it. So we pay no attention to what we're thinking and how it is affecting our behavior and performance. Understanding the importance of your thoughts, which give rise to emotions, is critical in changing your behavior. Managing your thinking and your emotions will lead to better management of your behavior. Remember, thoughts arouse emotions.

What is thinking?

Thinking is conscious and it's active. Think of it as internal speech (requires language). Sometimes that inner conversation appears to come unbidden or automatically; this would be subconscious thought. But it is during conscious and active thought that thinking takes on a whole new role. Here we can focus our thoughts to solve a problem. We can plan, design and, quite literally, create. This is where we can purposefully produce our thoughts and put some form to them. In simpler words, thinking is the action of using one's mind to produce thoughts.

90% of the people don't think

It's true; most people don't think. They go through their days on automatic, their thoughts being a reaction to what's happening around them and to them, rather than being a purposeful response. No wonder, though. The Socratic method is no longer taught in schools, and the young people of today don't seem to understand the importance of the "question." If you ask yourself (your mind) a question, the mind will always answer. Ask a great question, and you'll always get a great response. In fact, it's the act of questioning that creates our thoughts. So, think what will happen to a person who doesn't understand the importance of questions. Something happens, and random, or at least reactive, thoughts appear. Negative questions abound. *Why is this happening to me? What's going on? Who does he think he is? Where does this leave me?* Get the picture? What if this person had responded rather than reacted? The questions asked might appear like this: *This is interesting: how can what's happening serve me? Do I understand the situation properly, or will he clarify it for me? He certainly has some strong opinions: I wonder what his experience is in this area and if he would be interested in sharing his story and his reasoning? I think I'll ask him. Can't hurt, right?*

Why is this important?

The questions we ask will determine what we say and do. They are like the programs we feed our computer so that it can manipulate the raw data it receives in a way that is useful to us. You're the operator or programmer of your mind. You don't want to fall asleep on the job, do you? Then learn to ask yourself questions designed to get your mind used to generating specific words and actions so that they become a habit you can call on in many different situations. I call them rituals.

209

Thoughts arouse emotions

One of the most wonderful aspects of thought is that it can arouse emotions. You can discover which words or thoughts elicit emotions that can work for you in a difficult situation, then you can practice calling up those emotions. I'm talking about positive emotions like excitement, joy, happiness, and peace.

COMPETENCES OF EMOTIONAL INTELLIGENCE

There are many different views and opinions on the competences of Emotional Intelligence. I've found the following to be the best examples to describe the important competences.

Self-awareness is the foundation on which all other competences build on. Often, we don't take the time to disengage from day-to-day activity to review what has happened to us.

Example … Before you go to bed at night, take the time to review your day. Ask questions like: *What were the positives? Which of my goals were achieved? What happened to make the day memorable?* Once you feel your review is complete, set your mind to work, planning tomorrow's day. You should write your goals down.

Example … How can you really understand your stress levels if you don't spend some quiet time posing and answering questions designed to put your focus on the stress you feel in each large muscle mass? So, think back to a time when you felt totally relaxed and the stress literally bled from your body. What did that feel like? Compare that feeling to the one in the muscle mass we've been talking about. Clench those muscles for a count of ten and release. Does the feeling in the muscles match what you remembered? Not quite? Clench the muscles for another 10 seconds and release. Immediately notice how the muscles feel. Now do this with all the large muscles in your body, beginning with your head and working downward to your feet.

Make sure you're doing your best to match the feeling of relaxation you remembered. Breathe in when you clench, breathe out when you release. You can even pretend you're releasing the air through the muscle you just released. Do you feel yourself settling into your chair or your bed? Keep practicing and one day soon you'll find yourself completely relaxed.

Self-assessment is the ability to honestly assess one's strengths and weakness. This has to be done skillfully. It's an opportunity to review what you're naturally good at and what the opportunities are for self-improvement. Self-assessment does not mean beating yourself up! But, rather, it's thoughtful self-reflection that adds value in increasing your awareness about yourself and how you interact with your environment.

Again, use questions to elicit the thoughts you're after. *What did I do well today? What skills and talents did I use? What could I have done better? How?*

Managing Emotion

I've heard emotion referred to as a wild stallion that must be tamed. Thoughts generate emotions; emotions generate thoughts. Of the two possibilities, which seems more useful to you? Thoughts generating emotions, right? You have the reins: it's up to you to teach the stallion what that means, that you're in control.

It's much easier to choose useful thoughts that generate positive, supporting emotions than it is to control the thoughts evoked by powerful, negative emotions. Think about it … you always have a choice. You can ask questions that create thoughts that will evoke useful emotions or you can be overrun by thoughts that boil up unbidden from out of control negative emotion. You can tame the wild stallion or it can cast you into the dirt.

How is this emotion working for me? What thoughts can I choose that will evoke a better emotional response? What's good about this situation, and how can it serve me? Such questions are designed to focus on positive thoughts, emotions and results rather than reacting blindly to whatever emotion is elicited by the situation at hand.

Emotional Intelligence can be taught, improved and used within your company to achieve your goals. It is definitely a strong tool that can put you out in front of your competition. For more information or to book a seminar for your company, contact me at **ravsbains1@gmail.com**.

FINAL NOTE

The most important thing you can take away from this chapter is: **Life has no meaning other than what we give it**. A woman at a party stumbles and falls. One person is concerned that the woman might have been hurt by the fall. A second person starts laughing (because he noticed that the contents of the woman's drink flew into the face of someone he doesn't like very much).

In this situation, a woman fell. This has no meaning without context, hence the reactions of the two witnesses. They both put the fall into a specific context and then assigned meaning. The first witness saw the fall in the context of the woman becoming injured. This triggered the emotion of concern. The second witness saw the fall in the context of someone he disliked getting a drink in the face. This triggered the emotion of delight.

The trick, the wisdom we must develop, is understanding that we have FREE WILL to choose whatever it is we want to think, feel, say or do. It doesn't matter what has happened, because it means nothing until, and if, we make it so.

Remember ... "People will often forget what you said, but they will never forget how you made them feel." - Maya Angelou

To book a seminar for your organization, contact
Rav Bains at **ravsbains1@gmail.com**